Past Masters
General Editor Keith Thomas

Malthus

Donald Winch is Professor of the History of Economics at the University of Sussex. His previous publications include studies of classical political economy, the relationship of economics and policy during the twentieth century, *Adam Smith's Politics* (1978), and (with Stefan Collini and John Burrow) *That Noble Science of Politics* (1983).

Past Masters

AQUINAS Anthony Kenny
ARISTOTLE Jonathan Barnes
AUGUSTINE Henry Chadwick
BACH Denis Arnold
FRANCIS BACON Anthony Quinton
BAYLE Elisabeth Labrousse
BERGSON Leszek Kolakowski
BERKELEY J. O. Urmson
THE BUDDHA Michael Carrithers
BURKE C. B. Macpherson
CARLYLE A. L. Le Quesne
CERVANTES P. E. Russell
CHAUCER George Kane
CLAUSEWITZ Michael Howard
COBBETT Raymond Williams
COLERIDGE Richard Holmes
CONFUCIUS Raymond Dawson
DANTE George Holmes
DARWIN Jonathan Howard
DESCARTES Tom Sorell
DIDEROT Peter France
GEORGE ELIOT Rosemary Ashton
ENGELS Terrell Carver
GALILEO Stillman Drake
GIBBON J. W. Burrow
GOETHE T. J. Reed
HEGEL Peter Singer
HOMER Jasper Griffin
HUME A. J. Ayer

JESUS Humphrey Carpenter
KANT Roger Scruton
LAMARCK L. J. Jordanova
LEIBNIZ G. MacDonald Ross
LOCKE John Dunn
MACHIAVELLI Quentin Skinner
MALTHUS Donald Winch
MARX Peter Singer
MENDEL Vitezslav Orel
MILL William Thomas
MONTAIGNE Peter Burke
MONTESQUIEU Judith N. Shklar
THOMAS MORE Anthony Kenny
WILLIAM MORRIS Peter Stansky
MUHAMMAD Michael Cook
NEWMAN Owen Chadwick
PASCAL Alban Krailsheimer
PETRARCH Nicholas Mann
PLATO R. M. Hare
PROUST Derwent May
RUSKIN George P. Landow
SHAKESPEARE Germaine Greer
ADAM SMITH D. D. Raphael
SPINOZA Roger Scruton
TOLSTOY Henry Gifford
VICO Peter Burke
VIRGIL Jasper Griffin
WYCLIF Anthony Kenny

Forthcoming

ARNOLD Stefan Collini
BENTHAM John Dinwiddy
BLAKE Marilyn Butler
JOSEPH BUTLER R. G. Frey
COPERNICUS Owen Gingerich
DISRAELI John Vincent
ERASMUS James McConica
GODWIN Alan Ryan
HERZEN Aileen Kelly
HOBBES Richard Tuck
JEFFERSON Jack P. Greene
JOHNSON Pat Rogers
KIERKEGAARD Patrick Gardiner

LEONARDO E. H. Gombrich
LINNAEUS W. T. Stearn
NEWTON P. M. Rattansi
PAINE Mark Philp
ROUSSEAU Robert Wokler
RUSSELL John G. Slater
SCHILLER T. J. Reed
SOCRATES Bernard Williams
TOCQUEVILLE Larry Siedentop
WITTGENSTEIN A. C. Grayling
MARY WOLLSTONECRAFT
  William St Clair
and others

Donald Winch

Malthus DISCARDED

Oxford   New York
OXFORD UNIVERSITY PRESS
1987

Oxford University Press, Walton Street, Oxford OX2 6DP

Oxford New York Toronto
Delhi Bombay Calcutta Madras Karachi
Petaling Jaya Singapore Hong Kong Tokyo
Nairobi Dar es Salaam Cape Town
Melbourne Auckland

and associated companies in
Beirut Berlin Ibadan Nicosia

Oxford is a trade mark of Oxford University Press

British Library Cataloguing in Publication Data
Winch, Donald
Malthus—(Past masters).
1. Malthus, T. R.   2. Economics—Great
Britain—History—19th century
I. Title   II. Series
330.15'3   HB863
ISBN 0-19-287653-8
ISBN 0-19-287652-X Pbk

Library of Congress Cataloging in Publication Data
Winch, Donald.
Malthus.
(Past masters)
Bibliography: p.   Includes index.
1. Malthus, T. R. (Thomas Robert), 1766-1834.
I. Title.   II. Series.
HB863.W56 1987   330.15'3   87-11179
ISBN 0-19-287653-8
ISBN 0-19-287652-X (pbk.)

Typeset by Joshua Associates Limited, Oxford
Printed in Great Britain by
The Guernsey Press Ltd.
Guernsey, Channel Islands

In grateful memory of
Patricia James, 1917–87

Acknowledgements

I have been extremely fortunate in being able to call upon the knowledge of two of the leading Malthus scholars of our day, Patricia James and John Pullen, whose magnificent editions of the *Essay on Population* and the *Principles of Political Economy* have just appeared and will set a new standard in these matters after years of neglect. In addition to using these editions in draft form, I have also had the benefit of their comments on this foray into a subject on which they have both worked for many years. I am also grateful, as on so many occasions in the past, for the suggestions for improvement made by two friends, Stefan Collini and John Burrow, the latter still a colleague, the former, unfortunately, no longer so. Any remaining errors of fact, tact, and interpretation are my responsibility.

D. W.

Contents

Abbreviations

The following abbreviations are used when citing references in the text.

FE   The first edition of *An Essay on the Principle of Population* (1798) as reprinted in facsimile by Macmillan for the Royal Economic Society, edited by J. R. Bonar, 1926, reprinted 1966.

E   The sixth edition of *An Essay on the Principle of Population* in two volumes published in 1826.

Pr   *Principles of Political Economy*, Cambridge University Press for the Royal Economic Society, 1987, a variorum edition compiled and edited by J. M. Pullen in two volumes, the first of which contains the edition published in 1820.

P   *The Pamphlets of Thomas Robert Malthus*, Augustus M. Kelley, New York, 1970.

R   *The Works and Correspondence of David Ricardo*, Cambridge University Press for the Royal Economic Society, edited by Piero Sraffa and M. H. Dobb in eleven volumes, 1952–1973.

PJ   Patricia James, *Population Malthus; His Life and Times*, Routledge and Kegan Paul, London, 1979.

Q   Article on 'Political Economy', *Quarterly Review*, January, 1824, XXX, 214–334 as reprinted in *Occasional Papers of T. R. Malthus*, edited by B. Semmel, Burt Franklin, New York, 1963.

1 Reputation

Robert Malthus's name is chiefly and irrevocably linked with what he was the first to present as a universal and perpetual dilemma: he maintained that the prospects for permanent improvement in the condition of the mass of society in all countries was placed in a precarious balance by an unequal race between the hare of population growth and a tortoise representing the power to expand food production. 'Malthusian', as a result, has become a permanent part of our vocabulary, still much used in scientific and popular debate on the problems of population growth in the Third World, as well as by environmentalists who treat the balance between population and exhaustible resources as a global problem. But this book does not deal—except perhaps indirectly—with these twentieth-century dilemmas and the ways in which they have been or might be resolved. Its main focus will be on the man who, rightly or wrongly, has had his name attached to them. More especially it is concerned with the writings of Malthus (1766–1834) considered against the background, mostly in the late eighteenth century and first third of the nineteenth century, which first gave prominence and point to his ideas.

Treated as a practical demographer, as someone attempting to explain actual population trends in order to propose measures designed to achieve more desirable rates of population growth, the significance of Malthus's ideas lay primarily in their defeat of a long-standing tradition which had automatically linked a large and growing population with economic progress and national power. For Malthus, a large population might only be a reflection of earlier prosperity and a warning of imminent danger of falling living standards. After Malthus, therefore, the idea that rapid population growth was always desirable could never be upheld without an attempted rebuttal of his views; and in the process it was frequently overlooked that for Malthus too population growth could be advantageous under some circumstances. While evidence has subsequently accumulated to show that the hare has usually been far less swift than he supposed, and that the tortoise is capable of such a remarkable turn of speed in some countries that we are now embarrassed by food surpluses, Malthus is still recognized as having created the terrain over which demographic dispute continues to rage, forcing those who dislike or disagree with his conclusions to argue over issues which he was the first to dramatize.

Demography in the modern sense of the term, however, was never Malthus's sole concern, and it is certainly not the only reason for the persistent attention paid to his writings. From a broader, more political perspective, Malthus's main claim to fame, or notoriety, rests on his decisive attempt to undermine the doctrine of human perfectibility, and Utopian speculations of an egalitarian or communistic nature. He still serves as the figure most responsible for revealing the anxieties that are supposed to lie at the heart of political and economic liberalism. He marks the moment when optimism regarding the prospects for social improvement turned sour and fatalistic, serving to dampen hopes by reminding us of the narrow limits within which any progress is possible, with the result that his population theory has become the hallmark of all that is sombre and 'dismal' about the laws of political economy. Moreover, since one of the earliest conclusions which Malthus drew from his findings was a denial of the right of the poor to relief under the English Poor Laws, 'Malthusian' has become a byword for those harsh *laissez-faire* social policies which equated poverty with moral failing. A fear of falling in the social scale appeared to replace the opportunity to rise as the leading motive of men in society. Mass poverty and existing inequalities between rich and poor were seen as an indelible part of the human condition, capable only of being remedied by forms of individual prudence and self-help that were unlikely to be adopted or even to be available to the mass of society until their living standards had already risen.

As Malthus was only too well aware, we do not love the bringer of bad tidings, especially when the message concerns something as inherently controversial as family life and population. One has only to think of the enraged tone of twentieth-century debates on abortion and contraception to be reminded of this fact: members of the First World who recommend policies to control the growth of Third World populations run the risk of being charged with genocide. Malthus's position has probably generated more vituperation, vilification, and misunderstanding than that of any comparable figure in the history of social and political thought. It has driven many of those who have written about him into a defensive or apologetic stance from the outset, and his work continues to invite the rehearsal of moral outrage and superior humanity—an invitation many still find difficult to resist some one hundred and fifty years after his death.

One simple explanation for the misunderstanding and dislike provoked by Malthus lies in the sheer immodesty of his basic propositions. The principle which he enunciated with such force was a universal one, capable of explaining the past, present, and future condition of mankind, wherever it was to be found. Malthus did not claim to have discovered this principle—the idea that population expands up to the available subsistence was something of an eighteenth-century commonplace. But anyone who illustrates its operation with such thoroughness, emphasizing the vice and misery which it inevitably generates, must expect to arouse staunch counter-claims and to have his motives subjected to close scrutiny. From the outset too, the question of population was connected with a number of potentially inflammatory themes: the reasons for economic inequality; the role of self-interest as opposed to benevolence in human affairs; whether

3

man's destiny could be described as progressive or merely as a perpetual oscillation between narrow limits; the role of the passions, especially the passion between the sexes; whether man should for some crucial purposes be assimilated to the animal or botanical world, despite his capacity for free will and virtuous conduct—a formidable version of the ancient conflict between Nature and Culture. There was also, for a Christian civilization in which Malthus, himself an Anglican clergyman, was to become a significant figure, the major question of how belief in a benevolent deity could be squared with the existence of widespread poverty and misery that was only loosely or problematically connected with sinful conduct. Many of these moral questions are matters of life and death in the most literal sense, and it is one of the more interesting features of Malthus, and certainly one that will be stressed here, that he consistently attempted to combine the viewpoint of moralist and objective scientist.

The inherently explosive quality of the topic may help to explain, even if it does not excuse, the number of fundamental untruths about Malthus's views that were given currency during his lifetime. He was accused of being an enemy to all population growth; of proposing prohibitions on marriage by the poor; of maintaining that nothing should be done to reduce infant mortality or improve health standards; of recommending war, pestilence, and disease, and other forms of vice and misery as checks; of advocating immediate abolition of the right to assistance under the Poor Laws on the sole grounds that this was necessary in the interest of reducing the burden of poor rates on the rich; and of denigrating all forms of benevolence and private charity. In addition to being accused of currying favour with the rich by relieving their consciences about the poor, he was later to be charged with being the hired spokesman of the landed gentry when he spoke in favour of the Corn Laws, a measure which he thought would have a positive effect in raising food supplies and living standards.

After his death such charges were embellished by Marx and Engels, among others, and hence have continued to feature in the works of their followers up to the present day. Thus for Marx, Malthus represented all that was retrograde in bourgeois society. He was both a plagiarist and 'a bought advocate' who elevated the temporary historical laws of bourgeois society into eternal natural laws of the human condition. His ideological role lay in diverting the attention of the working class from the true reasons for its shameful condition under capitalism. It was the continual recruitment of the 'reserve army' by means of labour-saving technology that kept the labour market overstocked, rather than that 'insult' to the intelligence of the working class, the principle of population. The power of capital itself, rather than any attempt to regulate the supply of labour, was responsible for creating the conditions necessary for exploitation. 'A shameless sycophant of the ruling classes' was thereby added to charges of having, at one and the same time, put forward a set of truisms, and depicted human nature in degrading terms—charges levelled, often in vehement fashion, by such early critics of Malthus as William Cobbett, Samuel Taylor Coleridge, Robert Southey, William Hazlitt, and Thomas Carlyle.

The list of Malthus's admirers and converts is, however, equally long and impressive. These included many of the leading politicians of the day from the younger Pitt onwards, as well as most political economists, whether of a Christian or secular frame of mind. Malthus continued to answer those critics who maintained that he had perpetrated an elaborate blasphemy in calling God's word ('Be fruitful, and multiply') and beneficence into question, and he took pride in having converted William Paley—one of his teachers and the leading Anglican interpreter of the political and social order—to his views. After John Bird Sumner, later to be Archbishop of Canterbury, published his *Treatise on the Records of Creation* in 1816, a work specifically designed to show the 'consistency of the Principle of Population with the Wisdom and Goodness of the Deity', Malthusian ideas became a standard feature of the social teachings of the Established Church, attracting the interest of some leading evangelical intellectuals: Edward Copleston (Bishop of Llandaff), William Otter (Bishop of Chichester), and Richard Whateley (Archbishop of Dublin). It was also from the ranks of the divines that Malthus acquired his most fervent disciple in the shape of the Scottish preacher and professor Thomas Chalmers, whose sermons and prolific writings were probably responsible for more converts than anything Malthus himself ever wrote.

Many of those who approached political economy from a more secular perspective adopted Malthus's population principle as the foundation for their position on wages, the causes of poverty, and the need for fundamental changes in the Poor Law. This was especially true of David Ricardo, James Mill, and his precocious son, John Stuart Mill. The *Edinburgh Review*, the Whig organ which became the most important contemporary arena for rehearsing new ideas on political economy, and to which Malthus contributed several articles, consistently upheld his position and attacked that of his opponents. There were respectful criticisms of Malthus's priorities and way of expressing his principle from within the orthodox political economists' camp in the 1830s, notably by Nassau Senior, later to be one of the main authors of the Report of the Royal Commission on the Poor Laws in 1834; and what amounted to a retraction of his earlier support by John Ramsay McCulloch, another of Ricardo's followers. But John Stuart Mill, reviewing the situation in the 1840s, nearly half a century after Malthus's first writings on population, put up a stout defence of the population theory against its critics, treating it as the beginning of all sound thinking on the subject of wages and mass poverty: 'Though the assertion may be looked upon as a paradox, it is historically true, that only from that time has the economical condition of the labouring classes been regarded by thoughtful men as susceptible of permanent improvement.'

Mill's influence as the leading liberal philosopher and political economist of his day ensured a renewed lease of life for the Malthusian principle as the key to higher per capita incomes during the third quarter of the nineteenth century. But his use of control over population growth as a major criterion for judging the likely future success of socialist and communist alternatives to present society was representative of a new phase in the history of Malthusianism—a phase more accurately described as Neo-Malthusianism. For Mill, like his father before him, was an advocate of birth control within marriage, a solution which Malthus regarded as immoral and likely to diminish the sum of human happiness. Moreover, in Mill's hands, an argument which began life as an attack on the viability of communistic societies became associated with the case for social experiment along just those lines.

Malthus's population principle also acquired a new career when it was revealed that both Charles Darwin and Alfred Russel Wallace were indebted to their reading of Malthus for insight into the mechanisms underlying natural selection and the struggle for survival in the plant and animal kingdom, thereby setting on foot a complex interchange of ideas between the social and biological sciences. An argument based on human ecology, showing the adaptive response of human beings to variations in their environment, and making use of strategic comparisons with the biological and botanical world, was reappropriated by biology as part of an evolutionary perspective that had, or was taken to have, considerable significance for the study of social evolution.

Population and agriculture were Malthus's main point of entry into the larger issues posed by political economy, a field of inquiry that was still dominated by Adam Smith's *Wealth of Nations* when Malthus made his first contributions to the subject. For the first two decades of the nineteenth century he was the single most prominent figure in the development of the new science. In addition to making the problem of wages and food prices under conditions of economic growth central to what subsequently became known as classical political economy, he made original contributions to the fundamental laws which were held to underlie rent, profits, and capital accumulation.

In dealing with Malthus's reputation as a political economist it is important to recognize that he was addressing himself to a number of controversial questions in a historical context which gave them special point. Thus his first *Essay on Population* (1798) appeared in an atmosphere that was still dominated by the French Revolution and all that this *événement* entailed in terms of hopes of dramatic improvement in the human condition as a result of changed political institutions. It also appeared four years after and two years before two major periods of acute scarcity in the availability of grain, the price of which was the main determinant of the living standards of most wage-earning families. In 1801 the first of the decennial censuses appeared, revealing that British population, contrary to a common belief shared by Malthus, had been growing rapidly during the second half of the eighteenth century; it was to reach its maximum rate of increase during the period in which Malthus was producing successive editions of his *Essay*. The second and subsequent editions of the *Essay* (1803–1826) also appeared during the Napoleonic Wars and their aftermath, a period characterized by a puzzling combination of economic signals: the emergence of Britain as a dominant commercial and manufacturing power under conditions of economic warfare, rising taxation, and national indebtedness; a period in which agriculture enjoyed prosperity as a result of high food prices and rents, but when it was also becoming clear that Britain had become a net importer of foodstuffs and might only be able to support her growing population from domestic sources at ever-higher prices, and by acquiescing in the unprecedented shift of occupational pattern towards foreign trade, urban employments, and manufacturing. Above all, the signs of prosperity were accompanied by burgeoning expenditure under the

Poor Laws to support the growing numbers of able-bodied labourers requiring public relief. From almost every point of view, therefore, Malthus was responding to circumstances in which major and troubling structural changes in Britain's economic life were taking place; when fundamental choices were being posed between a future in which Britain might have to rely on manu- facturing strength, and hence capacity to export, to support a growing population, and one in which legislative intervention might be required to achieve a balance between agriculture and industry on moral, strategic, and economic grounds. Malthus was inclined towards the latter solution, and with hindsight we can see that he was, on the one hand, the crucial figure posing the dilemmas mentioned above, while on the other hand being, broadly speaking, on the losing side in the prolonged dispute which they occasioned.

The main challenge to Malthus's ideas on political economy came from David Ricardo, and much of the history of the subject during the first quarter of the nineteenth century is contained in the remarkable public and private disputes conducted by these two close friends. The controversy covered all the main laws or principles of the infant science and their application to the urgent policy questions of the day, with Ricardo gradually establishing ascendancy—partly by a narrower form of economic logic, and partly as a result of the proselytizing activities of his followers.

One of the recurrent topics in the Malthus–Ricardo dispute concerned the explanation for post-Napoleonic Wars distress. Malthus treated this as a problem of general glut or depression, attributable to a deficiency in 'effective demand', though his diagnosis was also bound up with longer-term issues connected with the maximum rate at which capital accumulation and growth could take place. Reviewing this dispute in the light of his own concerns with unemployment in the 1930s, John Maynard Keynes saw in Malthus a worthy predecessor whose attempts to counter Ricardian ideas mirrored his own struggle to escape from economic orthodoxy. Hence Keynes's remarkable conclusion that: 'If only Malthus, instead of Ricardo, had been the parent stem from which nineteenth-century economics proceeded, what a much wiser and richer place the world would be today!' Just as Malthus played a part in stimulating Darwin during the process which resulted in the *Origin of Species* (1859), so this different aspect of his work features in the story of Keynes's *General Theory of Employment, Interest, and Money* (1936).

Whatever the merits of Keynes's judgement, he was certainly correct in suggesting that if history is only to be written from the victors' point of view a good deal will be lost, not least from the victors' case, by not understanding how the choices were originally posed. The vicissitudes of Malthus's reputation will be reconsidered in the concluding chapter, after the evidence of what he was actually contending in his various writings has been reviewed and interpreted. But first we must consider the outline of his biography, trusting that his character and the nature of the man will gradually emerge from the ensuing treatment of his opinions.

2 Life

Malthus was born on 13 February 1766, the second son and sixth child of Daniel Malthus, a well-to-do, eccentric country gentleman with serious, if somewhat scattered intellectual enthusiasms which included science, foreign literature, botany, and a fervent admiration for the works and character of Jean-Jacques Rousseau. Robert was educated initially by a clergyman friend of his father, but at the age of 16 was sent to the Dissenting Academy at Warrington, where he lived with and was taught by Gilbert Wakefield, a leading and controversial figure in the Unitarian movement following his resignation from the Church of England in 1779. This was an unusual step for Malthus's father to take, for although his son was not the only pupil of Wakefield to come from an Anglican background, Robert was destined from an early age to take up a career in the Church of England. The decision to send him to be educated by Dissenters with 'advanced' views is an interesting sign of his father's own position, as well as being of some consequence to the son's writings later.

In 1784 Malthus went up to Jesus College, Cambridge, the college at which Wakefield had been a Fellow. Here, too, Robert's path crossed with Dissenters of a radical turn of mind: one of his tutors was William Frend, who, just after Malthus left Cambridge, was removed from his Fellowship for publishing an attack on the civil disabilities imposed on Dissenters by the Test Acts, as well as for opposing the war with the new French Republic.

Malthus's main studies at Cambridge centred on mathematics, and he emerged as Ninth Wrangler in 1788. Despite a speech defect resulting from a cleft palate, he was ordained immediately after leaving university, and first took up a curacy at Okewood near his family's home in Albury, Surrey. In 1793 he was elected to

11

a non-residential Fellowship at Jesus College. During the ten years that followed graduation, therefore, Malthus lived the quiet life of a country curate, carrying out the modest duties of his post, and completing what had already been a thorough yet leisurely education, while continuing to live with his parents and two unmarried sisters.

In 1796 Malthus made an abortive attempt to publish a political pamphlet entitled *The Crisis, a View of the Present State of Great Britain, by a Friend to the Constitution*. The recorded fragments of this provide a few valuable insights into Malthus's early opinions, but it was not until two years later that he managed to appear in print, though as yet anonymously, as the author of a work bearing the following title: *An Essay on the Principle of Population as it affects the future Improvement of Society, with Remarks on the Speculations of Mr. Godwin, M. Condorcet, and other Writers*. The book had humble domestic origins in a dispute with his Rousseauist father, but it was to catapult its 32-year old author into the limelight for the first time, and provide him with the subject which dominated his life and subsequent writings.

The success of what was essentially a polemical work dashed off in a fairly short time without access to many sources induced Malthus to make a more thorough investigation of the historical and demographic record in order to document his position more fully. Extended tours of Scandinavia in 1799, and of France and Switzerland in 1802, were partly undertaken in order to collect additional information on the subject of population. The result of these labours was the appearance in 1803 of a second and much enlarged edition of the *Essay on the Principle of Population* with a modified and more positive subtitle: *A View of Its Past and Present Effects on Human Happiness, with an Inquiry into our prospects respecting the Future Removal of the Evils which it Occasions*.

In the same year Malthus became Rector of Walesby in Lincolnshire, a permanent living from which he drew an income for the rest of his life. This enabled him to marry in 1804, at the age of 38; three children were born to a marriage which provided the peaceful domestic setting for the rest of Malthus's life. These facts may be of some significance when dealing with someone whose main solution to the population problem lay in deferred marriage. An equally important fact, however, was his appointment as Professor of History and Political Economy at the East India Company's College in Hertfordshire, established in 1805 for the training of boys aged 15 to 18 who wished to enter the Company's civil service. The appointment, the first of its kind in England, provided Malthus with an opportunity to make political economy his profession as well as his hobby. While this post conferred financial security, it was purchased at a heavy price in terms of the time and effort he frequently had to devote both to quelling riotous pupils and to the defence of the college's existence and autonomy against its numerous critics.

In his first *Essay*, when dealing with the contribution, as he saw it, of the English Poor Laws to the spread of pauperism, Malthus broached a policy question which was to become the chief focus of public debate on poverty in the period which led up to the Poor Law Amendment Act of 1834, an Act which he was widely considered to have god-fathered. He also contributed to a debate on another topic that was at the head of the agenda of political economy for the next three or four decades, when he published a pamphlet on the *High Price of Provisions* in 1800. In addition to producing successive editions of his *Essay* (six in all, the last appearing in 1826), he wrote topical pamphlets on the Corn Laws and the nature of rent, and articles on monetary problems and Ireland.

Although these publications established Malthus as one of the leading political economists of his day, he did not produce a comprehensive statement of his position on the principles of political economy until 1820. For some years he hoped to bring out an edition of Adam Smith's *Wealth of Nations* that would have incorporated the original ideas on political economy which

13

he had developed in the course of his teaching at the East India College. This project had to be abandoned in 1814 when a rival edition of Smith's classic appeared, the first of several opportunities to put his views before the public in a reasonably coherent form which Malthus either missed or mishandled—a fact which is of some significance to his reputation both then and later. Thus, while Malthus had by the end of the Napoleonic Wars in 1815 assembled in characteristically untidy fashion many of the ingredients for a distinctive set of Malthusian variations on Smithian themes, he was increasingly aware of growing divergences between his own theoretical and practical opinions and those of other political economists, notably Ricardo, with whom he had been in regular correspondence for a number of years. Ricardo had rapidly assimilated Malthus's theories of population and rent in his own contribution to the Corn Law debates in 1815, but he put them to quite different uses: first to attack, rather than defend the Corn Laws, and secondly, to construct a model of economic growth and distribution which was to provide the foundation for his *Principles of Political Economy* published in 1817, with further editions appearing in 1819 and 1823. From this point onward, therefore, Malthus found himself having to combine exposition of his own ideas with responses to those of Ricardo and his followers. His own version of the *Principles of Political Economy considered with a View to their Practical Application*, as well as two shorter books on the *Measure of Value* (1823), and *Definitions in Political Economy* (1827), became attempts to combat the theoretical and methodological presuppositions of Ricardo and the 'new school of political economy' which was being formed around Ricardo's ideas. Malthus died in 1834, having been only partially successful in this enterprise. The appearance of a posthumous second edition of his *Principles* in 1836 did little to revive a reputation that had been overshadowed by that of his friend. When John Stuart Mill undertook a comprehensive restatement of the principles of political economy in 1848, he did so along Ricardian lines, praising Malthus for his pioneering work on population, but otherwise treating him as someone who had unfortunately lent his authority to an error on a fundamental question, namely the possibility of general over-production.

As the remarks of Keynes cited at the end of the previous chapter indicate, this was by no means the final judgement on the subject. But the first question posed by Malthus's biography must be: how did this obscure and mild-mannered curate come to be the author of a work that was to scandalize so many people?

3 Population: the first *Essay*

The first *Essay*, as its subtitle makes clear, was designed as a contribution to the debate on 'the future improvement of society', and more especially as an answer to the visionary speculations of William Godwin and the Marquis de Condorcet on this subject. None of the fundamental issues raised by the debate was entirely novel: the innate characteristics of man as opposed to what could be attributed to his social circumstances and political institutions; whether his fate could be described as progressive or cyclical; the relationship between rich and poor in society; and whether population growth represented an insurmountable barrier to prospects for permanent social improvement—all this and much else that featured in the controversy had been rehearsed in detail by moral philosophers, theologians, and political speculators during the second half of the eighteenth century. But the debate which Malthus joined in 1798 had acquired heightened significance by virtue of the fact that Godwin's *Enquiry Concerning Political Justice* (1793) and Condorcet's *Esquisse d'un tableau historique des progrès de l'esprit humain* (1795) had appeared during the period of political upheaval initiated by the French Revolution.

In this respect Malthus's first entry into the lists can be compared with another famous contribution to the debate aroused by events in France, namely Burke's *Reflections on the Revolution in France* (1790). Indeed, many have seen Malthus's first *Essay* as an integral part of the campaign against pro-French or Jacobinical literature begun by Burke; as a counter-revolutionary tract for the times, delivering what is perhaps a more shattering blow to hopes of improvement in man's temporal fate through political reform than Burke's furious denunciation of those abstract thinkers who had brought such ruin on France and threatened to do the same in Britain. Both men certainly bequeathed to their successors powerful arguments in favour of the established order; and the antagonism which Burke aroused among radical circles in the 1790s was maintained against Malthus for a much longer period, and by critics drawn from a wider political spectrum which included 'romantic' conservatives and, later, socialists, as well as political radicals. When seen in this counter-revolutionary light, Malthus provides a far less defensive argument for the status quo than can be inferred from Burke's *Reflections*. The conservative forces appear to have gone onto a permanent offensive.

In a history of popular ideologies these similarities between Burke and Malthus have something to be said for them; but they do not prepare the reader for the stance adopted by Malthus in his *Essay*. For whereas Burke appeared in the guise of an enraged critic, Malthus presented himself as a calm and dispassionate seeker after scientific truth in the accepted Newtonian manner; as a friendly arbitrator in what he described as the 'unamicable contest' between those speculative philosophers who entertained dreams of unlimited improvement, and those advocates of the present order (he probably had Burke in mind) who defended abuses from a partisan perspective. Malthus spoke as one who 'ardently wished' to believe in the kind of improvements held out by Godwin and Condorcet, as someone who was 'warmed and delighted' by the portrait of man's future which they had painted. Unfortunately, his regard for scientific truth would not allow him to share their dreams. Since false hopes were being entertained on the basis of faulty diagnoses of the present state of affairs, he had reluctantly taken up his pen to oppose them.

This was not an ironical pose on Malthus's part. It consorts well with the origins of the first *Essay* in an argument with his father, and with the fact that Malthus, as a result of the peculiarities of his early education, was brought up within precisely those radical dissenting circles that were the target of much of Burke's anger and provided the background out of which Godwin's anarchistic, free-thinking, but anti-revolutionary work emerged. Malthus should also be regarded as a seeker after scientific truth because of, rather than despite, his clear theological commitments. Although his Cambridge education was aimed at producing a clergyman, this was tantamount, in the circumstances of the day, to producing a Newtonian natural and moral philosopher capable of subjecting all theories to the test of observation and experiment. Malthus's quest for a middle way between opposed doctrines, his search for the 'golden mean', and his respect for the claims of both abstract reason and experience were characteristic of the way in which he approached all subjects in his later writings. The first *Essay*, therefore, reveals a great deal about his later work, despite the changes that were later to be made to Malthus's opinions on population and related matters of political economy.

Although written hastily and published anonymously, the first *Essay* pursues a complex polemical strategy. It begins with an exposition of the principle of population treated as a set of deductive propositions; and it then proceeds to show how historical and empirical evidence lend support to the abstract principle. Secondly, the implications for egalitarian and perfectibilist schemes in general, and those of Condorcet and Godwin in particular, are spelled out in what also amounts to a short treatise on scientific method according to the accepted Newtonian model. Thirdly, an argument is mounted against Adam Smith's theory of economic growth which is of great significance to the later development of Malthus's views on political economy, and will therefore be considered in that context (Chapter 5). Fourthly, there is a concluding exercise in theodicy designed to show why the 'disheartening' results of the operation of the natural laws previously expounded are entirely compatible with belief in a beneficent deity. Though often treated as an embarrassing and detachable part of the *Essay*, this theodicy contains essential clues to the form of theological utilitarianism which underlies Malthus's moral philosophy.

The principle of population

Malthus took his stand on three propositions. First, that population cannot increase without the means of subsistence; second, that population invariably increases when the means of subsistence are available; and third, that 'the superior power of population cannot be checked without producing misery or vice' (FE 37). The first two of these propositions he took as established truths, with the reader being referred to the writings of David Hume, Adam Smith, and Robert Wallace on this point. His own contribution to the subject lay in drawing attention to the precise ways in which population growth had in fact been limited by the operation of a series of checks which entailed vice and misery in one form or another.

The deductive argument required two postulates: the necessity of food to man's existence, and the assumption that the passion between the sexes was both necessary 'and will remain nearly in its present state' (FE 11). Malthus also posited that the power of population to grow was 'indefinitely greater' than the power of the earth to produce subsistence. He illustrated this inequality by means of a contrast between the geometric power of population increase and the arithmetic power of improvements in food production. Applied to Britain in 1798, with an assumed population of 7 million (it was actually well over 10 million), the two series would look as follows: population had the power to double every twenty-five years (from 7 to 14 to 28 to 56 million by 1883), but food production could only increase by a constant factor (from 7 to 14 to 21 to 28, half the amount that would be needed to support the population in 1883). Since the two unequal powers must be equated in some way, one should look to the means by which the difficulty in acquiring subsistence constantly exerts a check on population—a check that must fall mainly on the great mass of mankind at the bottom of society's pyramid.

The checks came in two forms, positive and preventive. The former reveal themselves in higher mortality rates and lower life expectancy, the latter operate by means of voluntary restraint on birth-rates. Both entail misery and vice, misery being a necessary consequence, vice—a category designed to hold the casualties in the eternal struggle between good and evil—being a probable result. War, pestilence, and famine were the main positive checks; abortion, infanticide, prostitution, and other 'unnatural' attempts to accommodate the constant passion between the sexes while avoiding the consequences, counted as preventive checks. The principle of population, therefore, showed that no society, present or future, could guarantee that all its members 'should live in ease, happiness, and comparative leisure', feeling 'no anxiety about providing the means of subsistence for themselves and families' (FE 17).

Here was Malthus's dilemma locked in what he sometimes treated as an 'impregnable fortress' of Euclidian logic. He then proceeded to argue, as Rousseau and other eighteenth-century writers on the theme of inequality had done, from an assumed state of simpler and purer human nature. Let us imagine a state of equality, simple manners, and virtue, a state in which misery and vice were unknown. In such a state, population, through early marriage and reproduction uninhibited by any concern for rising or falling in the social scale, would increase at its maximum possible rate, a situation that could actually be observed in the United States where population doubled every twenty-five years. It might be possible to double the production of the means of subsistence in the first twenty-five years, but could it be quadrupled in the next, as would be required if population growth continued at the maximum? Clearly not, in Malthus's opinion. And since food was necessary to existence, a widening gap could not be allowed to develop. Long before this the positive and preventive checks would be at work keeping population down to subsistence. Nor was this proposition confined to isolated states that might gain temporary relief through emigration; the analysis could be extended to cover the globe as a whole.

In the world of plants and animals unrestricted increase was counterbalanced by overcrowding and failure of the excess to survive. In man the capacity for reason and foresight acted as a preventive check. Thus in the present state of society prudence would take account of such matters as the effect of marriage and reproduction on future independence and rank, the possible need to work harder, and the life-prospects of any offspring. In some respects, therefore, there had been progress and improvement on the earlier savage state, where the positive checks operated with full force. Despite such prudential considerations, however, population increase placed the lower classes of every society under constant pressure of want and distress as a result of food scarcity, falling wages, and increasing toil.

What Malthus had in mind was a form of cycle arising from delayed responses, periods of good times associated with high wages leading to early marriage and population increase, followed by bad times in which distress brings population increase to a halt. At the bottom of the cycle the cheapness of labour would act as an encouragement to food production, thereby restoring the balance between population and resources to the original position. It is a model of 'perpetual oscillation' rather than unilinear progress, and while it is possible for the oscillations to occur around a rising trend, there was no guarantee that this would be the case. The oscillatory path entails the persistence for the mass of misery and vice at some point in each of the cycles—'the same retrograde and progressive movements with respect to happiness are repeated' (FE 31).

Why then had these permanent rhythms gone unnoticed? Malthus's answer was that the phenomenon was probably more irregular in real life than his model suggested; that the histories of

21

mankind which had been written so far had largely concentrated on the higher classes, rather than on those whose lives were most subject to the cycles; and that in any case a proper study of the subject required 'the constant and minute attention of an observing mind during a long life' (FE 32). It entailed close attention to marriage rates, the incidence of 'vicious customs', the comparative mortality of the children born to the poor, and a general comparison of wages and the living standards of the poor over time. Moreover, the process would not be a regular one: it would be constantly spurred on or interrupted by causes of a more or less temporary nature—by agricultural and commercial success and failure; by wars and pestilence; by 'the invention of processes for shortening labour without the proportional extension of the market for the commodity' (FE 34); and by the way in which the movement of money wages usually lagged behind changes in the price of food. To this list Malthus added the operation of the Poor Laws, a subject which was later to occupy a good deal of his attention.

Malthus was quite right in believing that such an extended study of the empirical circumstances attending the lives of the mass of society had only just begun. A pioneering treatment of *The State of the Poor* by Sir William Morton Eden had appeared the year before Malthus's *Essay*, but the official decennial census of population did not begin until 1801. Nevertheless, Malthus's agenda gives a precise foretaste of his own inquiries and methods of procedure during the rest of his life.

The first *Essay* draws on simple ethnographic evidence to show that the principle of population operates among North American Indians and the Hottentots, as illustrated by the constant state of war and famine in which they lived, as well as by the hardships endured by their women. The idyll of the noble savage in a conjectured state of nature would be short-lived; and the actual state of savage man fell far short of nobility.

In modern Europe, where agricultural improvements had

occurred, population had grown; but in Malthus's opinion it had been growing at a slow rate (doubling over a period of 300 to 400 years). This could be accounted for by resort to the preventive check of delayed marriage by the middle and upper classes, and by the operation of both preventive and positive checks on the lower classes. Malthus drew attention to infant mortality rates and the stunted growth of children in rural England—subjects on which he could comment on the basis of his experience as a country curate. He also regarded the growth of 'unwholesome' manufacturing towns, with their crowded conditions and proneness to epidemics, as another sign of the operation of his principle. But the most striking evidence of the pressure being exerted by population in England was to be found in the growth of expenditure on poor relief, currently standing at about £3 million per annum. (It had doubled over the previous two decades and was to reach over £8 million by 1815.) In the short term, this redistribution from rich to poor, under conditions either of food scarcity or low elasticity of supply in response to price increases, merely increased the competition for available supplies. In the long term, the availability of relief as of right had the more disastrous effect of lowering wages and encouraging early marriage among those without the prospect of supporting children by their own efforts and income. Hence the conclusion that the Poor Laws 'in some measure create the poor which they maintain', and its corollary that 'dependent poverty ought to be held disgraceful' because '[a] labourer who marries without being able to support a family, may in some respects be considered as an enemy to all his fellow-labourers' (FE 86).

At this stage of his inquiry then, before any reliable census data was available, Malthus was inclined to believe that the British population was growing slowly and that, despite improvements in agriculture and the rise of manufacturing, standards of living or, more generally, 'happiness and virtue', had not improved greatly during the previous century—a conclusion which was, as we shall stress in a later chapter, in marked contrast with Adam Smith's far more optimistic account of the same phenomenon since 1688. Malthus agreed with Smith, however, in regarding the United States of America as peculiarly favoured by the abundance of cheap land and high wages, by the absence of tithes and other agricultural hindrances such as primogeniture, and by the possession of 'a greater degree of liberty and equality'. Here truly was an exception that proved the rule, a society where 'population increases exactly in the proportion that the two great checks to it, misery and vice, are removed; and [where] there is not a truer criterion of the happiness and innocence of a people, than the rapidity of their increase' (FE 107–8). Nevertheless, even new countries like America could not expect to escape indefinitely from the principle of population. A man 'might as reasonably expect to prevent a wife or mistress from growing old by never exposing her to the sun or air' (FE 343). As we shall see, however, Malthus recognised that while 'perpetual youth' could not be sustained, it was possible, through unwise policies, to produce a state of 'premature old age'.

The anti-utopian argument

In criticizing Condorcet and Godwin, Malthus naturally concentrated on those matters on which his opponents could be found in agreement: a broadly Rousseauist attribution of social evils to imperfections in man's political arrangements; a common assumption that reason, benevolence, and greater equality were likely to characterize the society of the future; and considerable convergence in their speculations on the subject of increased life expectancy and the remoteness and remediable nature of any future population problem. Malthus was fully justified in placing the works of Condorcet and Godwin side by side as evidence of a radical Enlightenment belief that, as a result of the French Revolution and 'the great and unlooked for discoveries that have taken place of late years in natural philosophy', high expectations were being entertained 'that we were touching on a period big with the most important changes that would in some measure be decisive of the future fate of mankind' (FE 2).

Condorcet and Godwin reflected another feature of post-Revolutionary thinking that can be attributed to the violent course of events after 1792. It was expressed by Godwin in the preface to a set of essays he published in 1797 under the title of *The Enquirer*. There he spoke of the early mood induced by 'the principles of Gallic republicanism' as one of 'exaltation and ferment', when 'the friends of innovation were somewhat imperious in their tone'. He wished to announce his retreat to a 'more patient and tranquil' position. Faced with a violent present reality, one might say, it was now necessary to sustain the original hopes released by the Revolution by calmer and more philosophical speculations on the prospects for a golden future that was to be achieved by peaceful means, through reason and sincerity. There are good grounds for believing that Condorcet, living closer to that violent reality, and becoming a victim of it when he died in prison in 1794, shared Godwin's aims.

But there are also differences between Condorcet and Godwin which can best be briefly expressed by saying that Condorcet's vision was more technocratic, emphasizing the role to be played by the application of scientific knowledge to the reconstruction of society from above, an aspect of the idea of progress which he passed on to his French successors, Saint Simon and Auguste Comte, the founders of nineteenth-century sociology constructed along positivist lines. Godwin's ideal society, by contrast, is informed by an anarchistic vision which rejects authority, even when benevolently constituted, and is more ambivalent in its attitude towards economic complexity and technical progress. Moreover, Godwin's work was a contribution to the British political debate provoked by French developments: an answer to Burke, but no less so to Thomas Paine and those impetuous 'friends of innovation' whose revolutionary ideas Godwin wished to repudiate along with Burke's defence of the aristocratic status quo. In these and other respects, Malthus was more closely engaged by Godwin than by Condorcet, and was sometimes to be found in agreement with him.

Godwin's Utopia was based on a belief that government, along with legal coercion and all deferential relationships that were not based on true merit, would gradually give way to a regime based on frankness, sincerity, simplicity, transparency, and respect for individuality and privacy. Vice was merely a species of ignorance. All those corrupt institutions which prevented man's natural goodness from manifesting itself would sink under the weight of their own imperfections in the face of enlightened opinion. All inequalities between rich and poor, the main sources of crime and civil disarray, would disappear, as would the alienating effects of the division of labour and a system whereby the many were enslaved by their need to labour in order to produce luxuries consumed only by the few. In a society where 'no man is to apply to his personal use more than his necessities require', mutual benevolence would replace more possessive forms of property, which included the institution of marriage. By eliminating the artificial wants associated with inequality, and by dividing the labour of the community more equally and simply, the working day could be reduced to less than two hours for all, thereby allowing attention to be focused on the disinterested pursuit of communal rather than individual welfare.

Godwin had fully anticipated the Malthusian objection before it had been penned by answering Robert Wallace's *Various Prospects of Mankind, Nature and Providence* (1761), a work upon which Malthus was later to draw. Wallace had advanced a Utopia based on common ownership, but had forecast that under a perfect system of government there would be no constraint on population growth, with the result that, at some future point, 'mankind would encrease so prodigiously, that the earth would at last be overstocked, and become unable to support its numerous inhabitants'. In the absence of any acceptable expedient for controlling population, Wallace concluded that his Utopia would destroy itself and force a return to 'the same calamitous condition as at present'. Godwin's answer to Wallace was that various checks would prevent population from increasing beyond the means of subsistence, some involving delayed marriage, others involving abortion, infanticide, and celibacy. But if these checks proved inadequate, three-quarters of the globe was still uninhabited and there was ample scope for agricultural improvement: 'Myriads of centuries of still increasing population may pass away, and the earth be yet found sufficient for the support of its inhabitants. It were idle therefore to conceive discouragement from so distant a contingency.'

With progress, too, 'mere animal function' would be replaced by more cerebral pleasures. Condorcet had addressed himself to this problem, but had suggested birth control as a solution rather than a waning of the passion between the sexes. To both of Malthus's opponents, then, population pressure was either a remote prospect or something that could easily be overcome when it arose. It was a distinctive mark of Malthus's interpretation of the problem, however, that it was 'imminent and immediate' rather than in the future. Moreover, most of the remedies mentioned by Condorcet and Godwin entailed recourse to expedients which Malthus regarded as examples of vice and misery.

Condorcet had speculated about 'organic perfectibility', a state that would be achieved through improvements in diet, medicine, and other physical changes in modes of life. While these would not abolish mortality, they could prolong life expectations indefinitely. Godwin's hopes for the prolongation of human life centred more on the enhancement of intellectual powers and the growing hegemony of mind over body. Such conjectures were an affront to the Newtonian in Malthus; they broke a fundamental rule of scientific inquiry by reasoning from causes to possible effects, rather than from observed effects to possible causes. They were a reversion to the 'wild and eccentric hypotheses of Descartes' (FE 159). Facts should not be made to bend to hypotheses, and Nature should not be treated as mutable. Malthus could see no evidence for indefinite life expectancy; the whole speculation was based on the fallacy that because the limits of human life were undefined, because they had increased in the past, therefore they could be extended almost at will. Malthus could not help thinking that his opponents, having rejected the religious promise of eternal life, had found it necessary to invent immortality on this earth as a compensation. He also defended belief in the immortality of the soul from the charge that it was mere conjecture on a par with the speculations he had rejected. On such matters, where no scientific authority could be derived from experience, reasoning from analogy was defensible. And if we saw around us so much evidence of a supernatural power, why should we not suppose this power to be capable of resurrecting the physical body? But it is perhaps a mark of Malthus's strong commitment to the Newtonian method that he concentrated most of his attack on matters that could be settled by recourse to experience rather than revelation.

Malthus treated Godwin with great courtesy as the author of 'the most beautiful and engaging' (FE 174) system of equality produced so far. One of the features most admired by Malthus was its reliance on benevolence and 'the unlimited exercise of private judgment' rather than on solutions imposed by the community at large. In these respects Godwin had been responsive to one of the main objections raised against earlier schemes of equality, namely that individual liberty of action and conscience had to be sacrificed to the egalitarian and communitarian ideal. Godwin himself had condemned Rousseau's invocation of 'civic religion' on these grounds, and Malthus and Godwin shared a belief that human dignity derived from self-exertion and the exercise of discretionary foresight in managing personal affairs—a mark perhaps of the common Dissenting origins of their views.

Godwin's 'great error', according to Malthus, lay in 'attributing almost all the vices and misery that are seen in civil society to human institutions' (FE 176). Even so, it is worth noting that Malthus does not deny Godwin's contention that *some* institutions prolong or worsen economic conditions. Although the rich were incapable of preventing the 'almost constant action of misery upon the great part of society', and even their elimination in a state of equality would bring no respite, Malthus acknowledged that the rich were sometimes guilty of 'unjust conspiracy' (FE 36) against the labouring poor. He also accepted that the abolition of primogeniture might bring benefits by equalizing property and increasing the number of agrarian proprietors; and he conceded that the present degree of inequality could not be justified. Clearly Malthus was driven by the logic of the dispute to give as much to his opponent's arguments as possible, while still denying the conclusion. But there seems no reason to believe that he was not expressing his own opinions in making these concessions, which form a prologue to the ingenious *reductio* he was to apply to Godwin's vision.

Let us suppose a society in which all men are equal and living in a state of healthy abundance and simplicity. The ease of gaining subsistence and forming early attachments, without the constraint of monogamy, would ensure a rapid growth of population. What happens when all land is under cultivation, and all improvements have been tried? Will the spirit of benevolence and co-operation survive? Once this situation arises, the 'mighty law of self-preservation' will reassert itself with a vengeance. Scarcity and questions of desert re-enter the picture. Benevolence can no longer be exercized out of superfluity, only out of necessities. The division of land and private property would have to be invented. Exchange would replace gift relationships. Men would be held responsible for the children they had fathered, and later

29

generations would come into a world in which everything had been appropriated. Those without property would have to offer their labour services to those with property, and accept that what they were offered depended on a demand/supply relationship based on the food surplus and the available number of workers. This outcome would not be the result of depravity but of 'inevitable laws of nature', and the end result would be a return to the fundamental features of existing society, a 'society divided into a class of proprietors, and a class of labourers, and with self-love for the main-spring of the great machine' (FE 207).

Much of Malthus's negative critique is couched in terms of this demonstration that Godwin's scheme, whereby unnecessary labour would be abolished and labour divided equally, was incapable of being realized on a permanent basis. However, a more assertive position was also being advanced which can be understood initially as a decisive, though in itself hardly novel, attack on Rousseau's argument against civilization and the corrupting effects of property, inequality, self-interest, and vanity. Here again, though, Malthus started from a position that was close to that adopted by Godwin, who had also rejected Rousseau's invocation of the savage state as an ideal. Godwin attributed Rousseau's error to his decision to invert an infamous paradox, originally propounded by Bernard de Mandeville, whereby the advantages of civilized life (public benefits) were inextricably linked with individual pursuit of the objects of luxury and vanity (private vices). Godwin agreed thus far with Mandeville in believing that luxury and inequality was a state through which it was necessary to pass on the way to a higher form of social organization: 'But though inequality were necessary as the prelude to civilization, it is not necessary to its support. We may throw down the scaffolding, when the edifice is complete.'

It was this form of the critique of the status quo that Malthus set out to undermine with the following riposte:

It is to the established administration of property, and to the apparently narrow principle of self-love, that we are indebted for all the noblest exertions of human genius, all the finer and more delicate emotions of the soul, for everything, indeed, that distinguishes the civilized, from the savage state; and no sufficient change has as yet taken place in the nature of civilized man, to enable us to say, that he either is, or ever will be, in a state, when he may safely throw down the ladder by which he has risen to this eminence. (FE 286–7)

Malthus was answering Godwin by recourse to arguments derived from Adam Smith's more philosophically and morally respectable version of Mandeville's arguments on the connections between private vice and public benefit: his demonstration that under a system of free barter and exchange, self-love and social good could be reconciled; and that liberty, and material and cultural progress were best served by prudence and accumulation. Godwin had attacked Smith indirectly when he rejected the 'system of optimism', whereby 'seeming discords' were held to contribute to 'the admirable harmony and magnificence of the whole', and 'the intellectual improvement and enlargement we witness and hope for' was treated as 'worth purchasing at the expense of partial injustice and distress'.

Malthus simply inverted Godwin's claims by commending Smith's system of natural liberty as the only practical way of reducing inequality and dividing the necessary labour of society without employing force or having recourse to unacceptable forms of dependence. On this matter at least, Malthus was united with Condorcet, who had also endorsed Smith's system and conceded that the society of the future would still be dependent on those who maintained themselves by the sale of their labour. Acceptance of this lay behind Condorcet's proposals for a compulsory system of public insurance designed to iron out any inequalities arising from this source. Nevertheless, it is important to stress an earlier point, namely that Malthus did not proceed to give an optimistic account of man's present and future prospects.

His defence of Smith on the question of self-love was in fact to be an overture to an attack on a central feature of the *Wealth of Nations*—where, paradoxically, Malthus remained close to Godwin in doubting whether economic growth was always advantageous to the mass of society.

Another of Godwin's faults, according to Malthus, lay in his over-emphasis on the intellectual as opposed to corporeal elements in man's nature, his faith that reason and truth would always prevail over man's vices and moral weaknesses. Malthus held that many of the influences which affect moral character could not be controlled; they are beyond our will. Our efforts to improve might grow stronger, but we shall not succeed in eliminating vice. Godwin had conjectured that the passion between the sexes, like all inferior passions, would wane. Malthus took the view that pure love and the sensual pleasures connected with it neither could nor should be ousted by intellectual pursuits. The latter, like any single source of pleasure, were equally subject to exhaustion or diminishing returns, and he closed this argument with one of his more pessimistic predictions, namely that 'the principal argument of this essay tends to place in a strong point of view, the improbability, that the lower classes of people in any country, should ever be sufficiently free from want and labour, to attain any high degree of intellectual improvement' (FE 217–18). How large this group would be, and under what circumstances members of the lower classes could be released from this condition, was to occupy a great deal of Malthus's attention in later editions of the *Essay*.

From Nature up to Nature's God

The 'melancholy hue' of the *Essay*'s conclusions led Malthus on, or rather back, to more fundamental questions of natural theology in a pair of concluding chapters outlining a theodicy capable of reconciling divine general providence with the existence of 'partial evils' associated with population pressure. Although some of Malthus's arguments in this theodicy departed from contemporary Anglican orthodoxy, the methodological underpinnings of the exercise conformed both with the Newtonianism of eighteenth-century natural theology, and the established principles of Anglican social apologetics. Society, no less than the physical and biological universe, was the creation of natural laws established by God with man's ultimate welfare in view. Hence the obligation to 'reason from nature up to nature's God, and not to presume to reason from God to nature'. Malthus had already charged Condorcet and Godwin with not following this precept when they speculated about 'why some things are not otherwise, instead of endeavouring to account for them, as they are' (FE 350).

Malthus maintained that this world should be seen as one in which man has been placed under the pressure of want in order to 'awaken inert, chaotic matter, into spirit' (FE 353). The wants of the body are the first stimulants to action, and necessity is the mother of invention, overcoming the listlessness that would otherwise prove destructive of improvement. Without the pressure of population upon subsistence, man would never have left the savage state; and if the pressure could ever be permanently abated, man would sink back into a state of torpor and lose all the advantages of civilization. The argument relies on a form of theological utilitarianism, proximately derived from the work of William Paley, in which pain-avoidance, as much as active pleasure-seeking, becomes the motor force of action. Pain and pleasure have their moral equivalents in the avoidance of evil and the pursuit of goodness. Moreover, when Malthus maintained that 'evil seems to be necessary to create exertion; and exertion seems evidently necessary to create mind' (FE 360), he was, once more, simply inverting one of Godwin's arguments to the effect that only savages were 'subject to the weakness of indolence'. In a civilized society, he held, 'it is thought, acuteness of disquisition, and ardour of pursuit that set the corporeal faculties at work'.

Malthus was countering this mind-over-matter view with one suggesting that mind could only develop out of matter.

Malthus believed that fixed laws of nature constituted the only means by which God's progressive purpose could be achieved on earth. If God was treated as a visible presence, capable of intervening to adjust the application of laws to specific circumstances in order to mitigate their effects, the incentives to industry and the exercise of reason, foresight, and intelligence would weaken. When applied to the variety of the human condition, in which some individuals and societies were less favoured than others, fixed laws were bound to produce partial evils. But it was folly to wish that all could be placed in some medium state of climate, fertility, and prosperity. All parts were necessary to the whole, as the roots and branches of a tree were necessary to its more useful trunk. It followed that our duty lay in finding ways of reducing the incidence of evil and poverty without weakening the system as a whole. And what was true of the different parts of the globe was also true of each society: 'If no man could hope to rise, or fear to fall, in society; if industry did not bring with it its reward, and idleness its punishment, the middle parts would not certainly be what they now are' (FE 369).

Here then was the basis for a more assertive case for the established order than that contained in Malthus's *reductio*. It was not sufficient to rely, as Godwin did, on the 'enlarged motives' that could only operate in exceptional cases. 'Narrow motives' were required to inspire action on the part of mankind taken generally. Just as sorrows and distress are necessary 'to soften and humanize the heart, to awaken social sympathy', so 'moral evil is absolutely necessary to the production of moral excellence' (FE 375). A perfect, uniform, and undiversified state, containing only good, would not bring forth our active powers of mind and character: 'Evil exists in the world, not to create despair, but activity. We are not patiently to submit to it, but to exert ourselves to avoid it' (FE 395).

Acting on the advice of more senior members of the Church of England, Malthus later withdrew some of the more heterodox elements in this theodicy. Nevertheless, it expresses views which constantly recur in his writings and are essential to an understanding of the peculiarities and paradoxes of his position as a social scientist and moralist. He provided the basis on which the principle of population could be incorporated within the Anglican tradition by such theologians as John Bird Sumner; and the terms on which this was accomplished help to explain why Malthus did not regard himself as being guilty of cosmic pessimism and would have been affronted by the connotations of such phrases as the 'Malthusian devil'. A natural law based on natural instincts could only be the work of a beneficent deity. Far from being a sombre and pessimistic reflection on the entire human condition, the population principle pointed out the means by which God intended to secure the happiness of the mass of society on this earth, and achieve a progressive development in man's mental and material condition. Paradoxically, therefore, Malthus's theological commitments provide him with a teleology of improvement that acts as the religious equivalent of the secular perfectibilism which his *Essay* set out to undermine.

4 Population: the second *Essay*

The two-volume version of the *Essay* that emerged in 1803 as a result of Malthus's travels and search for additional ethnographic and statistical evidence to illustrate the principle of population, was in many respects, as he claimed, a 'new work'. Although everything continued to revolve around the population principle, the expanded version was also a more mature treatise on morals and politics, expounding Malthus's hopes as well as fears about the course on which British society appeared to be embarked. The alterations made to the second *Essay* over the period 1803 to 1826 provide a running commentary on Malthus's intellectual development; they embody his responses to numerous critics and his efforts to encompass events and new evidence. This chapter and its successor will deal with the more important themes to emerge from Malthus's revisions of his basic position.

Freed from the constraints imposed by the earlier polemic, Malthus was now anxious 'to soften some of the harshest conclusions' of his original statement of the consequences of the population principle. The most important change was a reclassification of the checks to population designed to focus on moral restraint as the acceptable alternative to vice within the category of preventive checks operating on birth rates. Although Malthus had acknowledged the role of prudence or foresight in the first *Essay*, moral restraint was now given considerable prominence as the ultimate solution, the response that should be actively fostered. Other forms of prudential restraint might be accompanied by vicious practices, but moral restraint meant 'restraint from marriage from prudential motives, with a conduct strictly moral during the period of this restraint' (E I 15). It meant refraining from or postponing marriage on grounds of the likely effect on the economic and social status of having to support a family, accompanied by what French commentators have called *le célibat vertueux* during the waiting period. It defines the ideal moral response to population pressure, even though, as a realistic moralist, Malthus was fully aware that less-than-ideal prudential responses were likely to be more common.

Others have argued that the entire framework of the second *Essay* was changed by the dropping of the concluding theological chapters. But it is a mistake to believe that Malthus abandoned the brand of theological utilitarianism contained in his earlier theodicy in order to become a more secular social theorist; there was no conflict between Malthus the Christian moral philosopher and Malthus the scientist. The retention of the categories of vice and virtue, alongside, indeed attached to, pain and happiness, testify to their continuing importance. Indeed, an understanding of what precisely was 'moral' about moral restraint requires constant reference to the methodological standpoint of the theological utilitarian, for whom the greatest surplus of virtue and happiness over vice and misery was the supreme criterion for judging the worth of individual actions and social outcomes.

As the reference in the subtitle of the second *Essay* to 'the future removal or mitigation of the evils' occasioned by the operation of the principle of population suggests, a great deal more space is devoted to positive solutions. In other words, even though the basic model of human motivation remains intact, together with its reliance on the spur of material necessity, greater scope is allowed to human agency and legislative prudence in mitigating its results. This trend towards giving a human power greater scope over a natural power is a persistent feature of Malthus's later revisions and writings.

One of the more controversial legislative reforms espoused by Malthus was the abolition of the Poor Laws. The subject had been broached in the first *Essay*, and it became one of Malthus's major preoccupations in subsequent editions. When taken in conjunction with moral restraint, it has led many to accept the proposition that the main tenet of Malthusian social policy is that there should be no social policy—a position that seems to echo or anticipate such well-known ideas as the Protestant work ethic, the virtues of 'self-help', even the 'survival of the fittest' and the attribution of poverty to defects of individual character. As we shall see, Malthus's views on the Poor Laws are a good deal more complex than his long term aim of abolition suggests, and while moral restraint emphasizes individual responsibility as the most dignified and effective solution to pauperism, Malthus was far too closely identified with the Enlightenment belief in the application to social affairs of general laws of a Newtonian variety to subscribe to the view that poverty was visited only on the feckless. We also need to broaden the rather anachronistic notion of *social* policy to encompass political questions connected with education and civil and political liberties which were of particular importance to Malthus.

Moral restraint

Having uncovered a natural law which operated without exception on human affairs, Malthus saw the task of the Christian moralist as one of pointing out ways of minimizing its unfortunate consequences and maximizing its benefits both to individuals and society at large. But as with all problems of maximization or minimization, marginal adjustments rather than simple all-or-nothing choices were entailed. Every non-Utopian solution to the problems posed by population pressure involved striking a difficult balance between vice and virtue, and frequently between the lesser of two vices. In addition, short-term gains or losses had to be set against long-term results.

As in the first *Essay*, Malthus treated all universal passions, impulses and wants, when considered abstractly or generally, as being natural or good; the satisfaction of such passions brought happiness. The desire to satisfy our material wants was also the impulse which underlay the process of civilization itself, and the passion between the sexes was the foundation on which the pleasures associated with conjugal affection, a prime softening agency, was based. The danger to happiness lay not in these impulses but in the 'fatal extravagances' to which they gave rise. Since it was impossible to weaken the force of our basic impulses without injuring our happiness, regulation and redirection, rather than Calvinistic suppression or diminution, was the correct response.

The utilitarian view stresses the need to weigh the mixture of good and evil consequences flowing from an action rather than the motive for action itself. In the face of population pressure man's task was to conduct himself in a manner that would mitigate the evil consequences that accompanied the benefits derived from any general law of nature. Malthus traced once more the trail of misery and vice left by the failure to check birth rates: low wages, excessive toil, indigence, irregularity of employment, loss of character, crime, vicious practices, and high mortality rates. Hence the moral duty of delaying marriage until there was a prospect of supporting children. Celibacy for a longer period would, he felt, ease relations between the sexes and enable them to establish 'kindred dispositions' before marriage. The passion between the sexes would not be extinguished, but would burn 'with a brighter, purer, and steadier flame' (E II 274). The period of delayed gratification would become a period of sobriety, industry, and economy undertaken with marriage as its prize.

Malthus envisaged a quite different form of late marriage from that which he regarded as prevailing in his own time, namely arranged marriages between those with 'exhausted' constitutions and affections, chiefly undertaken for the sake of men. Women, presumed to be the more virtuous half of society, would adjust to the new system more readily, with the normal age of marriage rising to 28 or 30, depending on circumstances. Malthus recognized that later marriage might lead to an increase in the vices connected with sex, particularly on the part of men. He held that prostitution was always attended by evil because it weakened 'the best affections of the heart' and tended 'to degrade the female character' (E I 14). But the sexual vices were by no means the only vices, and they had to be compared with those arising from mass poverty. Thus prudential restraint, accompanied by vice, was preferable to misery and premature death. Although a more secular age may find it strange that Malthus seems to have ranked contraception within marriage as equal to, or even above, prostitution in the scale of vices, he does not appear to have been a prude in sexual matters. Nor does it seem accurate to attribute to him responsibility for narrowing the term 'moral' to connote sexual morality alone. It was only after 1817 that he substituted a weaker 'there may' in the opening part of the following sentence: 'I have little doubt that there have been some irregular connections with women, which have added to the happiness of both parties, and have injured no one' (E I 17). But while such liaisons might not produce misery for the individuals concerned, the utilitarian perspective required them to be described as vicious because their general effect was 'to injure the happiness of society'.

Moral restraint was the solution 'dictated by the light of nature, and expressly enjoined by revealed religion' (E II 281). The difficulties in acting according to these dictates, as in similar cases where temptation had to be overcome, could not serve as an argument against the duty they embodied. Nor was it necessary for moral restraint to 'be universally or even generally practised': partial implementation would be accompanied by improvement in the circumstances of those who practised it, thereby reducing the sum total of misery and vice. This explains why Malthus did not regard his ideal solution as tantalizingly Utopian (one could substitute 'Godwinian'): moral restraint did not entail acting from unaccustomed motives directed at a general good 'which we may not distinctly comprehend, or the effect of which may be weakened by distance and diffusion'. Each individual, acting without co-operation and aiming only at his own happiness, would also serve the general good: 'Every step tells. He who performs his duty faithfully will reap the full fruits of it, whatever may be the number of others who fail' (E II 285). It was a duty capable of being understood by all, even those of the 'humblest capacity'; and it placed responsibility where it belonged, on the person who produces children he cannot support.

Malthus did acknowledge, however, that a process of re-education directed at all classes, but especially those prone to fall from a state of poverty to pauperism, was required. He continued to attack those critics who focused exclusively on unjust political institutions, the avarice of the rich, and inequalities in wealth as the only causes of poverty, and kept up his attack on visionary doctrines of equality and common property in all subsequent editions of the *Essay*, adding Robert Owen's communitarian schemes in the 1817 edition. The lower classes could be brought to understand that they were the authors of their own fate, provided that efforts, such as his own, were made to overcome the influence of the doctrine that early marriage and large families conferred a public benefit. Malthus also attached considerable importance to public support for education both along general lines and in order to inculcate the truth of the principle of population: 'it cannot be said that any fair experiment has been made with the understandings of the common people' (E II 287). While this remained the case, 'the errors of the labouring classes of society [were] always entitled to great indulgence and con-sideration' (E II 41). They did not deserve to have their condition dismissed simply as the result of personal improvidence and want of industry.

The object of those who wished to better the condition of the poor must be 'to raise the relative proportion between the price of labour and the price of provisions'. Existing policies had merely

41

increased population and reduced real wages. Moral restraint offered a means of putting the hare of population growth to sleep, thereby giving the tortoise of food production a chance of first catching up, and then overtaking it. By such means Malthus hoped that it would be possible to inaugurate an era in which population growth would always lag behind improvements in food supply, uniting what he described as 'the two grand *desiderata*, a great actual population, and a state of society in which squalid poverty and dependence are comparatively but little known; two objects which are far from being incompatible' (E II 291). Wages would rise and poverty of an 'abject' kind would be entirely confined to those 'who had fallen into misfortunes against which no prudence or foresight could provide' (E II 272). In common with most of his contemporaries, Malthus was chiefly concerned with the number of able-bodied poor who were in receipt of relief; he might have had a more sympathetic hearing if he had always stressed the distinction between them and widows and the infirm—those whose situation could not be imputed to lack of foresight.

We find here too Malthus's answer to those who charged him with advocating a stationary or declining population. If the rate of increase could be slowed and then kept in step with provisions, he could 'easily conceive, that this country with a proper direction of national industry, might, in the course of some centuries, contain two or three times its present population, and yet, every man in the kingdom be much better fed and clothed than he is at present' (E II 293).

The Poor Laws

In the first *Essay* Malthus had argued that the Poor Laws, by attempting to guarantee a minimum level of support to all those whose income fell short of that necessary to support them and their families during periods of food scarcity and high prices, had contributed to the problem they were designed to alleviate by lowering wages, increasing the price of food, and encouraging population increase. He concluded that 'if the poor-laws had never existed, though there might have been a few more instances of very severe distress, yet the aggregate mass of happiness among the common people would have been much greater than it is at present' (FE 94). Here was another case where a balance of probabilities had to be struck, bearing in mind that on a strictly numerical basis, the lower, and hence most numerous classes, constituted 'the most important part of the human race'.

On these grounds Malthus criticized Pitt's plan to reform the Poor Laws in 1796, which would have granted relief on grounds of family size. But in 1798 Malthus's main proposals were: the abolition of the Settlement Laws, which restricted relief to those born within the parish, a policy for creating a free market in labour which had been advocated by Adam Smith in 1776; the granting of 'premiums' to those who took new land under cultivation; the removal of restrictions which kept agricultural wages artificially below those paid to urban artisans; and the establishment of county workhouses where assistance could be granted to those suffering from 'severe distress', regardless of nationality or place of residence, but on condition that work was undertaken at the going market rate.

Malthus's analysis of the unfavourable consequences of the Poor Laws rested on the assumption of fixity, or extreme inelasticity, of food supply, an assumption that was more or less valid under conditions of acute grain scarcity, when the domestic harvest fell short of what was needed to maintain existing standards of food consumption. Over the longer run Malthus conceded that the additional demand for food would act as a spur to food production, though at this point he introduced another assumption concerning the difference between food and 'wrought commodities'. Food supply was limited by the availability of fertile land and the length of time required for agricultural investments to come to fruition.

43

Moreover, the long run was not relevant to those suffering from high prices now.

In 1800, in a pamphlet addressed to the causes of the *High Price of Provisions*, and partly designed to carry on Adam Smith's campaign to show that dealers in corn were not responsible for exacerbating scarcity, Malthus returned to the Poor Laws by adducing the recently introduced 'allowance system' as one of the reasons why grain prices had risen higher than they might otherwise have done on grounds of scarcity alone. The granting of assistance according to the gap between money wages and the cost of supporting a family at existing food prices merely placed extra purchasing power in the hands of poor families and enabled them to bid up the price of a fixed stock of food both to themselves and others not in receipt of assistance. Nevertheless, while reiterating his opposition to the Poor Laws in general, Malthus believed that in the special circumstances of the day the allowance system had been 'advantageous to the country' (P 19). By raising prices, the pressure of scarcity had implicated the whole community and brought about a general retrenchment in the use of grain. A higher price had also led to importation and greater incentives to farmers to increase next year's crop. But the episode also confirmed the diagnosis of the first *Essay*, namely that population was the underlying cause of vulnerability to periods of distress.

In the second *Essay* Malthus devoted several chapters to the subject, charging once more that the Poor Laws had alleviated individual misfortune at the expense of spreading 'the evil over a much larger surface' (E II 63). The defensible short-run features of the system were precisely those that produced the long-term drawbacks. As in his pamphlet on scarcity, he regarded the events of the previous years as confirmation of his original position. Attempts to maintain previous consumption standards under conditions of absolute scarcity had resulted in a far higher rise in prices than would have occurred if some effort had been made to economize in consumption. The brunt of the problem had fallen on those whose resources were just sufficient to make them ineligible for parish assistance, a group that was presumed to possess 'superior skill and industry' (E II 70). The additional £7 million which had been distributed as relief in 1801 was the main reason for the threefold increase in the price of grain. A permanent upward spiral had been avoided by the fact that the increase in money supply needed to support the inflationary process had come from the country banks, rather than the Bank of England. The return of peace and exceptional harvests had also reduced the need for assistance on the scale reached in earlier years. Raising wages in line with food prices would have had a more permanently damaging effect by increasing unemployment, especially in non-agricultural pursuits. Once more, however, Malthus made it clear that he was not opposing assistance: temporary aid was essential, and so were special importation and economy measures.

For Malthus's strong argument it was not only necessary to assume inelasticity in food supplies but also to maintain that in the long run the Poor Laws had encouraged population growth by encouraging early marriage and raising the birth rate. However, he acknowledged that the facts did not bear him out on this matter. Despite the unique provision of relief as of right, England did not seem to enjoy high birth and marriage rates when compared with other countries without such poor laws. Malthus attributed this to the fortunate persistence among the English poor of habits of independence and foresight which made them unwilling to rely on poor relief. Prudential if not moral restraint had come to the rescue. Adam Smith's 'desire of bettering our condition', or more relevantly, 'our fear of making it worse', was acting as a natural physic. Moreover, since each parish was obliged to maintain its own poor, those who paid the poor rates had an incentive to pull down cottages, thereby discouraging early marriage. The stringent conditions under which relief was granted also acted as a deterrent. Malthus was not contradicting his earlier support for the abolition of the Settlement Laws; he was merely pointing out that the existing system had features that were self-regulating.

On the question of workhouses, however, there was a change of position. In the second *Essay* he argued that attempts to employ the poor had failed, and where successful had driven non-parish labour out of business. No new capital was being brought into trade; it was merely being diverted from productive uses elsewhere. But he remained unwilling to press general principles too far, and so hedged his bets by saying that he could imagine circumstances in which the individual good derived from employing the poor in workhouses might over-balance the general evil.

Successive editions of the *Essay* enabled Malthus to claim that his views had been vindicated by events following the end of the Napoleonic Wars. It had proved impossible to maintain and keep all claimants in employment. The Poor Laws had not even prevented starvation, and those parishes which had been unable to cope with the demand on their rates had found it necessary to resort to voluntary charity. The poor were still being deluded by the false promises held out by the Poor Law statutes.

In the additions made to the *Essay* in 1817 and after, Malthus increasingly called upon an economic diagnosis based on cyclical deficiencies in 'effective demand' to explain recurrent bouts of distress—a diagnosis which will be considered more fully in a later chapter. The years following the peace settlement were certainly marked by severe unemployment and trade depression, which in turn were accompanied by violence and agitation for parliamentary reform. In the aftermath of the 'Peterloo massacre' in 1819, Malthus praised those who had helped to alleviate distress, and was certainly not pressing for abolition of the Poor Laws at this stage:

It is practicable to mitigate the violence and relieve the severe pressure of the present distress, so as to carry the sufferers through to better times, though even this can only be done at the expense of some sacrifices, not merely of the rich, but of other classes of the poor. But it is impracticable by any exertions, either individual or national, to restore at once that brisk demand for commodities and labour which has been lost by events, that, however they may have originated, are now beyond the power of control. (E II 99)

Malthus's ameliorative solution, once more, was a programme of public works, but designed this time not to compete with existing capital: road and bridge construction, and railway and canal preparation, plus some employment on the land fell into this category. Such measures would still entail disadvantage to others via the redistribution of capital, but he was willing to face up to this on the basis of a straightforward utilitarian calculus, and on the assumption that the measures would be temporary. As in the case of the steps taken to deal with scarcity in 1800, it was justifiable to spread the burden over a larger surface 'in order that its violence on particular parts may be so mitigated as to be made bearable by all' (E II 101).

During the post-war period Malthus also revised his earlier assessment of emigration as a 'very weak palliative' attended by dangers that it would merely create a vacuum into which increased population would flow. In 1817 it became a legitimate temporary device for coping with the depressed state of demand for labour. Malthus expected that the revival of effective demand after the war, taken in conjunction with a fall in marriage and birth rates, would restore full employment at good wages. Looking back on his prediction in 1826, however, he admitted that he had been proved wrong. Despite trade revival and the fall in food prices, there had been no decline in the proportion of the labouring classes needing parish support. Unlike some of his contemporaries among the political economists, Malthus was not prepared to advocate lower taxes and reduced government expenditure as a means of dealing with unemployment. Under some circumstances, he maintained, government expenditure provided a greater stimulus to demand than the same funds would have done in private hands.

But the persistence of the problem brought Malthus back to his earlier diagnosis of the role being played by population and the Poor Laws. The allowance system had prevented wages from rising in step with the price of provisions: '. . . no human efforts can keep up the price of day-labour so as to enable a man to support on his earnings a family of moderate size, so long as those who have more than two children are considered as having a valid claim to parish assistance' (E II 107). Hence his return to 'the *gradual* and *very gradual* [his emphasis] abolition of the poor laws', ('so gradual as not to affect any individuals at present alive, or who will be born within the next two years'), (E II 109) as the only long-term means of raising wages and preventing large sections of the population falling into pauperism. Cautious as ever, Malthus attached another condition to the proposal: 'I should be very sorry to see any legislative regulation founded on the plan I have proposed, till the higher and middle classes were generally convinced of its necessity, and till the poor themselves could be made to understand that they had purchased their right to a provision by law, by too great and extensive a sacrifice of their liberty and happiness' (P 34). And if this condition was not met, as he plainly did not think it was in the 1820s, he was prepared to settle for 'an improved administration of our actual laws, together with a more general system of education and moral superintendance' (PJ 450).

Political agency

Malthus's caution with regard to legislative change, as we shall see in later chapters, was not connected with his polemical attempts in the first *Essay* to minimize the role played by human institutions in explaining the persistence of vice and misery. What 'appear to be the obvious and obtrusive causes of much mischief to mankind', he had said in 1798, were in reality 'mere feathers that float on the surface' (FE 177). By 1803 this image had been removed, one of a number of minor changes which indicate that Malthus wished to allow greater scope to institutions and human agency as ameliorating factors in dealing with man's moral condition.

Morals were often linked with politics by Malthus, where this connoted something more philosophically ambitious than mere party allegiance. In terms of party labels, Malthus must be firmly placed in the Whig camp—though at a time when the Whigs were divided into a number of factions, and alliances were fluid, this is not a particularly enlightening ascription. Judging his position from the fragmentary quotations from his unpublished pamphlet on *The Crisis* written in 1796, it would seem that he was then a Foxite Whig, opposed to the repressive measures taken by the Pitt Ministry to curb the pro-French, anti-war, and reformist activities of the radical corresponding societies. Malthus's Whig credentials can also be gauged from his support for Catholic emancipation, the abolition of the public disabilities attached to membership of a Dissenting sect, and from the pattern of his friendships, which included the founders of the *Edinburgh Review*, the Whig quarterly. These Whig allegiances were to survive Malthus's defection from the free trade camp over the Corn Laws, and they enabled him to welcome, albeit retrospectively, the passage of the Reform Bill of 1832.

But the nature of Malthus's Whig sympathies cannot be judged from private alliances and public measures alone. In *The Crisis* he called upon 'the country gentlemen and middle classes' to revive 'true Whig principles' by acting as an independent influence, mediating between the Pitt Ministry and the claims of the popular radicals outside Parliament. In this way he hoped that a 'safe and enlightened policy' would be pursued, namely one of 'removing the weight of objections to our constitution by diminishing the truth of them'. In the same pamphlet, and on much the same grounds, Malthus advocated the removal of civil disabilities affecting Dissenters. He was well aware, from his acquaintance with the writings of his ex-tutors, Wakefield and Frend, that radical Dissenters were prominent in the campaign against the war with France. A policy of religious tolerance would, he hoped, do much to reconcile them to the Constitution: 'Admitted to equal advantages, and separated by no distinct interests, they could have no motives peculiar to themselves for dislike to the government.'

The role of moderate reformer, anxious to mediate between executive tyranny and popular radicalism, attempting to preserve the space which would allow gradual reformation to be achieved, defines the political stance which Malthus adopted throughout his life. It was a stance that entailed a lasting sensitivity to the radical Dissenting voice, while at the same time holding 'patriotic' views on the virtuous contribution which independent 'country gentlemen' had made in the past, and could still make to the preservation of English liberties. The main threat to these liberties lay in the growth of executive power, supported in Parliament by those with official and other connections with the ministry. The antidote lay in the preservation of balance between the various orders and interests represented in Parliament, and more especially in the hands of the independent members, supported by enlightened opinion in the nation at large, and acting as a check on executive encroachment. Malthus managed to add a 'modern' Whig position (of the kind associated with the name of Macaulay in the period before and after the Reform Bill) to what was an older 'Country' Whig tradition by linking the middle classes with the country gentlemen, and by according them a more prominent role over time.

The clearest version of this position can be found in a chapter in the second *Essay*, to which another was added in 1817, debating the following question: '[whether] a doctrine which attributes the greatest part of the sufferings of the lower classes of society exclusively to themselves, is unfavourable to the cause of liberty, as affording a tempting opportunity to governments of oppressing their subjects at pleasure, and laying the whole blame on the laws of nature and the imprudence of the poor' (E II 311). In other words, was Malthus's own view of poverty compatible with ideas on civil and political liberty which he also espoused? The way in which the question is framed reveals Malthus's underlying concerns and does a great deal to explain the persistence of his opposition to radical doctrines and schemes of equality.

Any failure to assign the correct causes of distress among the lower classes of society, by treating it as a simple product of misrule, Malthus argued, provided opportunities for revolutionary demagogues to bring down governments, and in turn to be brought down themselves when events proved that they too were incapable of meeting popular expectations. In an effort to end the cycle of anarchy 'the majority of well-disposed people, finding that a government, with proper restrictions, was unable to support itself against the revolutionary spirit, and weary and exhausted with perpetual change' (E II 312) would place themselves under the control of the tyrant or despot. Malthus's diagnosis of the way in which popular discontent, mob violence, and despotism were connected draws on classical commonplaces supplemented by Hume's ideas on the possible euthanasia, or 'easiest death', of the British Constitution in absolute monarchy. But the course of events in France after the Revolution, when taken in conjunction with the repressive measures adopted by British governments during the war, and the frequent eruption of popular unrest connected with food scarcity, machine-breaking, and post-war unemployment, gave renewed significance both to Hume's ideas and Malthus's diagnosis.

Echoing a century or more of anti-executive rhetoric, Malthus

51

announced himself to be 'an enemy to large standing armies'; and in 1817 he declared that the British government had 'shown no great love of peace and liberty during the last twenty-five years' (E II 330). The abolition of wars resulting from competition for land and food was one of the incidental benefits that would come from recognition of the principle of population. It would also deprive ambitious politicians of offensive weapons in the form of a ready supply of soldiers: 'A recruiting sergeant always prays for a bad harvest, and a want of employment, or, in other words, a redundant population' (E II 278). One of Robert Southey's many complaints against Malthus was the effect of his teachings on this subject: 'As if we did not at the moment want men for our battles!' He was also quite right to suspect, when writing to a fellow-Tory in 1808, that 'Malthus will prove a peacemonger'.

The dilemma of Malthus's position was shared by all those who felt themselves to be caught between the extremes represented by 'general declaimers' exploiting the genuine distress and ignorance of the unpropertied mass on one side, and the upholders of executive tyranny on the other. Malthus was surely speaking directly for himself when he said that the real effect of 'indiscriminate and wholesale accusations against governments' was 'to add a weight of talents and principles to the prevailing power which it never would have received otherwise' (E II 323). Regrettably, the standing army had proved necessary during the food riots which occurred at the turn of the century, and the threat of mob violence, rather than corruption, explained why the country gentlemen, 'the appointed guardians of British liberty', had so often found themselves supporting the Crown against the people during and after the Napoleonic Wars.

The political importance of the principle of population and the lessons it taught on the true causes of, and remedies for low wages and poverty lay in its effect in undermining the support given to 'turbulent and discontented men in the middle classes of society'. For with the fear of the mob removed, 'the tyranny of government could not stand a moment' (E II 322). Necessary reforms in the Constitution could be undertaken, and proper attention could be given to the 'striking and incontestable' contribution that better government could make to human improvement. Thus while the effect of constitutional reforms on economic problems could only be 'indirect and slow', Malthus was in no doubt that a combination of civil and political liberty, fortified by an extension of educational opportunities to the populace at large through a parochial school system along the lines advocated by Adam Smith, would act as a powerful means of spreading to the lower classes all those virtues of industry, respectability, independence, and prudence which had so far been confined to the middle classes.

In espousing *embourgeoisement* as a political and economic goal for the mass of society, Malthus may not have been particularly original, even in the early 1800s, though his views on education, religious tolerance, and political representation were probably far more common among Dissenting ministers than among Anglican clergymen at that time. Of possibly greater interest is the contrast with the more 'melancholy' reflections on the same subject in the polemical first *Essay*, and the fact that Malthus, when faced with arguments by others which stressed prospective *embourgeoisement* as a reason for expecting population pressure to recede, tended to revert to his original position—the one that found endorsement in his theology. This stressed the enduring part played by the spur of necessity in God's scheme of things, and made it difficult for Malthus to accept as whole-heartedly as others did that similar results might be achieved by forethought based on anticipated as opposed to established gains. His unwillingness to countenance birth control, as well as his scepticism towards such measures as emigration considered as a long-term solution, have a similar origin.

5 From population to political economy

Malthus's interest in population had its origins in a dispute over perfectibilism and the moral and political consequences of inequality and mass poverty, but he was quickly drawn into the ambit of Adam Smith's wider speculations on the wealth of nations—those questions of economic circulation, growth, and stability which were to remain central to classical political economy until the last third of the nineteenth century. On all these matters Malthus was to sustain a distinctive, sometimes isolated, position; and as a result of the way in which he entered this domain, namely in the course of an inquiry into the relationship between increased food production and population growth, there was always an aspect of his thinking which will have to be loosely described for the moment as an agrarian bias.

As population theorist, he was, after all, as much concerned with the possibilities (and difficulties) of expanding food production as with containing population growth; and his supposition that, once land had become scarce, food production could only expand at an arithmetic rate implied a version of what became known as the law of diminishing returns—an empirical or historical generalization thought to have special relevance to agriculture, which could be extrapolated into the future under certain assumptions about technical change and improvements in agricultural organization. Malthus's name was to become as closely associated with this law or tendency as any other contemporary political economist's; and his writings are replete with references to the peculiarities of agricultural production and the special difficulties under which it operated in attempting to absorb investment and respond to market stimuli.

But the starkness of the contrast between the arithmetic and geometric ratios of food and population, though useful in dramatizing the operation of checks and limits, tends to conceal another important feature of Malthus's thinking on all subjects: his 'doctrine of proportions', the search for *optimal* conditions or relationships, that 'golden mean' or precise balance of forces which would produce the best result under changing circumstances. Malthus expressed this concern in such homely analogies as that involving the hare and the tortoise, but he put it more precisely when he called upon his knowledge, acquired as a Cambridge mathematician, of calculus or the theory of fluxions: 'Many of the questions both in morals and politics seem to be of the nature of the problems *de maximus et minimis* in Fluxions; in which there is always a point where a certain effect is the greatest, while on the other side of the point it gradually diminishes' (P 119). Such an approach required distrust of solutions which appeared to depend on unidirectional change in any single variable. As he put it in another homely expression, 'there is no argument so frequently and obviously fallacious as that which infers that what is good to a certain extent is good to any extent' (E II 200).

Thus, while much of the polemical force of Malthus's first *Essay* derived from its emphasis on the crude physical limits posed by food supplies, it soon became apparent that the problems of agricultural production were intimately bound up with the other variables that underlay economic growth, notably capital accumulation, the relationship between agriculture, manufacturing, and foreign trade, and the connections between rents, profits, and wages, and the prices of goods and services. In moving from population theory to political economy, therefore, Malthus moved from the optimal relationship between food and population growth over time to a larger question involving the most desirable course that economic growth and the occupational pattern of the British economy should take.

While this describes the broad direction taken, it does not

55

capture some of the special features of Malthus's approach. It may not be surprising to find that the systematic theories of morals and politics which he deployed in dealing with population were carried over into his contributions to the narrower and, as Malthus saw it, subordinate field of political economy, though his practice in this regard was increasingly out of tune with that of many of his fellow-economists. Malthus was also more persistent in following Smith's example in attempting to place his interpretation of British economic problems against a comparative-historical background which brings out the plural emphasis of any inquiry into the wealth of nations. Furthermore, he remained closer to the political and cultural themes expounded by Smith in his historical treatment 'of the different progress of opulence in different nations', which dealt with the mutual interaction of town and country, manufacturing and agriculture, showing it to be essential not simply to economic growth, but to the 'silent revolution' which had overthrown feudal society in Western Europe, and which had placed liberty, defined as security under the rule of law and the disappearance of dependent relations between individuals and ranks, within the grasp of the majority for the first time.

Again, Malthus's attachment to these wider features of eighteenth-century debate on the origins of modern commercial or civil society, these attempts to establish the connections between commerce, 'luxury', and manufacturing on one side, and liberty, independence, national power, and political stability on the other, was also increasingly uncommon among his contemporaries. Such features formed part of a general inquiry into the benefits and drawbacks of modern civilized society when compared with its agrarian or feudal predecessors; and while improvement or progress provided an underlying motif, this did not rule out concern with possible 'seeds of decay'—sources of potential stagnation and decline. As political economy became more closely focused on the urgent, often short-term problems plaguing British policy-makers during the first quarter of the nineteenth century, such matters came to be seen, perhaps, as irrelevant or unproblematic by the new generation of economic commentators. This was never Malthus's position.

The sources and meaning of Malthus's agrarian bias are usually sought in more obvious places. In the course of developing his mature position, Malthus sometimes appeared to be questioning Smith's dismissal of those ideas, normally associated with his French predecessors, the *Economistes* or Physiocrats, which gave priority or special prominence to agriculture as the source of a nation's wealth and power. Malthus certainly returned to some of the issues which had featured in Smith's modifications to the Physiocratic conception of the relationship between agriculture, commerce, and manufacturing in the process of circular economic flow and growth. Smith had replied to the Physiocratic emphasis on the uniquely 'productive' qualities of agriculture by extending the term to cover all activities, including commerce and manufacturing, in which labour was employed productively by capital. The return on capital—interest and profits—thereby became, like rent, a source of economic surplus potentially available for future accumulation and economic growth. Malthus had no quarrel with this conclusion, but he did entertain serious doubts about Smith's stress on the universal benefits and self-regulating qualities of the process of capital accumulation, especially when the notion of the invisible hand was taken up in more doctrinaire form by other followers of Smith.

The most obvious mark of Malthus's agrarian sympathies, however, is normally taken to be his support for the Corn Laws, his defence of agricultural protection as a legitimate exception to the principles of free trade. In the eyes of many of his readers, even some of his friends, this established his reputation as an apologist for agricultural interests, especially those of the land-owning aristocracy. This reputation was compounded later when he maintained, on the basis of his theory of effective demand, that

57

the 'unproductive' expenditure of those in receipt of rent incomes might be necessary to sustain full employment and economic stability. The elements were thereby assembled for a portrait of Malthus as the ideological spokesman for an agrarian order increasingly under threat from industrialization and free trade.

The precise nature of Malthus's agrarian bias, and the way in which he developed his position, will be considered here. The story begins with a pair of chapters in the first *Essay* (16 and 17) which were enlarged to four and later six chapters in subsequent editions (Book III 8–13). These comprise a self-contained treatise on the optimal relationship between agriculture and manufacturing under different national circumstances; and they provide important clues to the final position adopted by Malthus on a number of key topics in political economy. They also furnish the background to his controversial decision to come out more firmly and publicly in favour of agricultural protection in 1815.

Agriculture versus manufacturing

In the first *Essay* Malthus employed the self-interest principle and Smith's system of natural liberty to counter Godwin's Utopian ideas, but he was not prepared to endorse Smith's optimistic views on the consequences of economic growth. Indeed, his initial foray into this territory consisted of a major attack on one of Smith's main conclusions—the idea that capital accumulation, in itself, could always be presumed to confer material benefits on society at large. According to Smith, these would accrue chiefly in the form of an expanding demand for labour, higher money wages, increased per capita output, and lower prices of those goods on which wages were mostly spent. Malthus questioned this essentially smooth account of the growth process by taking a polar case in which capital accumulation was applied solely to the employment of labour in manufacturing. While this might raise wages and be counted, on Smith's definition, as an increase in annual riches, the output of agricultural products would remain static. In such circumstances the rise of wages would be accompanied by an increase in the price of food, the main wage-good, thereby depriving the labouring classes of any improvement in real living standards.

Malthus was also casting doubt on Smith's interpretation of the historical record, his assessment that economic growth in Britain since the Revolution of 1688 had bettered the condition of the mass of society. According to Malthus the concentration of investment in trade and manufacturing had meant that wealth had been increasing faster than 'the effectual funds for the maintenance of labour'. Wealth was not, therefore, increasing the happiness of the mass by improving their condition. 'They have not, I believe, a greater command of the necessaries and conveniences of life; and a much greater proportion of them, than at the period of the revolution, is employed in manufactures, and crowded together in close and unwholesome rooms' (FE 313). Hence his belief, in 1798, that population had been increasing very slowly throughout the eighteenth century due to the equally slow increase in domestic food production. The rise in money wages had preceded the rise in the price of food, thereby raising costs ahead of revenues and impairing the ability of domestic agriculture to respond to the price rise. Enclosure and other improvements in agricultural technology had mostly been concentrated on grazing rather than arable wheat production, and fewer people were now employed on the land. In short, population would have increased faster if manufacturing and commerce had not expanded so rapidly at the expense of agriculture.

By means of such arguments Malthus sought to emphasize the possibilities of conflict between economic growth and the 'happiness and comfort of the lower orders of society'. Real wages might not increase and many wage-earners might suffer in the process of exchanging a stable and healthy form of life in agriculture for an 'unwholesome' existence in manufacturing occupations and towns, where they were exposed to the risks of vice and unhealthy surroundings as well as to greater uncertainties 'arising from the capricious taste of man, the accidents of war, and other causes' (FE 310). As Malthus said of manufacturing occupations in the first *Essay*, 'I do not reckon myself a very determined friend to them', (FE 293) and while he became distinctly friendlier towards them over time, this was a case where the conclusions of his science of morals took precedence over the science of wealth narrowly conceived. If vice and misery could be reduced by slowing down the growth of manufacturing, this should be made part of the moral calculus, even if it entailed lower per capita incomes on aggregate.

Malthus was proposing a major qualification to Smith's system of natural liberty, and doing so along lines that supported the Physiocratic conclusion concerning the priority, or especially 'productive' qualities, of food production. The chain of reasoning which he employed, however, was his own. He was suggesting that while investment in manufacturing might be advantageous to individual capitalists, it was less so to society—the reverse being true of agriculture. This opened up the possibility of socially-beneficial intervention by the government, though in the first *Essay* Malthus did not spell out what form this might take, apart from some hints that 'superior encouragement' had been given to commerce and manufacturing.

It is important, however, not to confuse Malthus's emphasis on the priority of agriculture and what would now be called the 'social' costs of industrialization with the position adopted by, say, his 'romantic' critics, Coleridge and Southey, who despised the commercial spirit of the age and entertained both feudal and bucolic visions. The social costs might be remediable (Malthus certainly noted improvements on this front in later writings), and the balance between agriculture and manufacturing might also, with greater difficulty, be adjusted in the right direction. Moreover, as a good Whig, albeit one with 'Country' sympathies which emphasized the beneficial oppositional role played by 'independent country gentlemen', Malthus was as conscious of the wider social and political benefits associated with the rise of commerce and manufacturing as Smith had been earlier:

Yet though the condition of the individual employed in common manufacturing labour is not by any means desirable, most of the effects of manufactures and commerce on the general state of society are in the highest degree beneficial. They infuse fresh life and activity into all classes of the state, afford opportunities for the inferior orders to rise by personal merit and exertion, and stimulate the higher orders to depend for distinction upon other grounds than mere rank and riches. They excite invention, encourage science and the useful arts, spread intelligence and spirit, inspire taste for conveniences and comforts among the labouring classes; and, above all, give a new and happier structure to society, by increasing the proportion of the middle classes, that body on which the liberty, public spirit and good government of every country must mainly depend. (P 118)

In the second and subsequent editions of the *Essay* Malthus's position on agriculture versus manufacturing underwent considerable development—so much so that he entertained the notion of publishing as a separate work the six chapters on the subject which eventually appeared in the 1817 edition. The flirtations with Physiocratic categories and definitions introduced in 1798 and extended in 1803 were largely excised three years later. But an expanded treatment was given to the comparative and historical dimensions of the issue in order to focus on the peculiarities of a 'large landed nation', such as Britain, experiencing a rapid shift towards commerce and manufacturing under conditions of war. Many of the negative remarks on manufacturing occupations were qualified or withdrawn, but Malthus made an additional effort to articulate his anxieties concerning possible sources of long-term stagnation arising out of the course on which the British economy was now fully embarked. Finally, the policy implications of his position,

61

particularly with regard to agricultural protection, were spelled out more openly.

In 1798 Malthus was inclined to believe that population had been rising very slowly throughout the eighteenth century. The census evidence which became available after 1801 made it necessary for him to recognize that population was rising quite rapidly. He also had to come to terms with the evidence that Britain had not only ceased to be a net exporter of grain products, but was on the verge of becoming a consistent net importer— a situation fraught with both short- and long-term dangers, especially under conditions of war. Indeed, the fact that Britain was almost continually at war with France until 1815 was a major consideration in Malthus's thinking. Napoleon's attempted economic blockade gave added point to worries about security in food supply. War had also imparted an 'artificial' stimulus to her commercial and manufacturing capacity by conferring near-monopoly status on many of her exports.

According to Malthus's new diagnosis, Britain had been an agricultural nation until the middle of the previous century, and everything would have proceeded smoothly if trade and manufacturing had grown at the same rate as agriculture. No 'germ of decay' (E 1803 ed. II 443) could be found in such a system of balanced growth. But Britain was becoming a predominantly commercial nation, and one mark of this was the recurrence of food scarcity and the need to import a larger proportion of her food needs in response to rising population and higher wages. He did not believe it was possible or desirable for a 'large landed nation' to adopt food importation as a long-run expedient. The short-term cost would be a rise in food prices in line with wages, and in the long term this would place a limit on the capacity to support a larger population. But the real danger to future prospects lay in the fact that economic pre-eminence based on commerce and manufacturing could be eroded through competition from newly industrializing nations. As the examples of

Holland, Hamburg and Venice showed: 'In the history of the world, the nations whose wealth has been derived principally from manufactures and commerce, have been perfectly ephemeral beings, compared with those, the basis of whose wealth has been agriculture' (E 1803 ed. II 437). Malthus was adding a new twist to the argument between ancients and moderns on the question of whether 'luxuries' were inimical or beneficial to a nation's survival: he was endorsing the position of the moderns, but maintaining that, carried to excess in the way he had diagnosed, dependence on manufacturing could contain 'seeds of decay', even though it might take a couple of centuries or more for them to develop.

The argument involved Malthus's doctrine of proportions. Conceding that commerce and manufacturing provided a market for agriculture, and hence a necessary stimulus to food production, he was seeking to define the point at which the growth of manufacturing could become excessive. Under war conditions Britain seemed to be approaching that point, with capital being attracted away from agricultural improvements by a combination of high profits in manufacturing, high interest rates due to war loans, and the slow and risky returns on capital employed in agriculture—factors which impaired the capacity of domestic agriculture to respond to the rise in wages and food prices. Any attempt to deal with the problem through cheaper food imports would further damage agriculture without much prospect of reducing money wages, which Malthus believed to be fairly inflexible in a downward direction.

The solution favoured by Malthus was a return to the situation in which Britain possessed the capacity to produce on a stable basis more than was normally consumed at home. Since he had shown that normal market processes did not produce the optimal solution, he was forced to conclude that a departure from Smith's free-trade principles was called for in order to deal with the fact that 'the body politick is in an artificial, and in some degree, diseased state, with one of its principal members out of proportion to the rest' (E 1803 ed. II 450). The expedients he favoured from 1803 onwards were a bounty on corn exports and restrictions on corn imports. This meant that he had to overthrow Smith's arguments on this subject which suggested that such measures would have no effect in raising agricultural profits and hence production. He also had to face up to the fact that agricultural protection might retard the progress of manufacturing, and he did so quite openly by accepting that it was desirable 'to sacrifice a small portion of present riches, in order to attain a greater degree of security, independence, and permanent prosperity' (E 1806 ed. II 257).

The mature version of Malthus's position on the relative merits of agricultural, commercial and manufacturing, and mixed societies can be found in the fifth and sixth editions of the *Essay* (1817, 1826) and in his *Principles of Political Economy* (1820), where the comparative dimension was further developed to the point where it became the framework for a treatise on nations classified according to the degree of their dependence on agriculture or manufacturing, and the different stages which they occupied in the development process. For example, the existing state of such 'feudal' economies as that of Poland, Russia, and Turkey provided ample material for speculation centring on the causes of agrarian stagnation, where the causes lay in their failure to have undergone the 'silent revolution' described by Smith when dealing with the political and economic benefits attributable to the opening up of commerce between town and country. Ireland, which was increasingly to occupy the attention of Malthus as the most striking and potentially dangerous contemporary illustration of the principle of population, provided a case of rapid population increase based on the ease with which subsistence derived from potato cultivation could be acquired. This situation was compounded by political and religious difficulties, and the lack of alternative employment in commerce and manufacturing. The contrast with a far more prosperous America, another agrarian state also undergoing rapid population growth, was obvious when placed within the new Malthusian framework.

Britain, however, still occupied the polar position as a nation with a growing population and the capacity, unlike Holland or Venice, of growing its own food, but increasingly reliant on commerce and manufacturing to support its population. Malthus continued to uphold the virtues of balanced growth, the dangers of dependence on unstable manufacturing activities, and the risks of forfeiting manufacturing pre-eminence to latecomers with greater capacity to support their populations from domestic sources. But while the limits of progress were never far from his mind, there were also signs of an increasing accommodation to the contemporary facts of British economic life and the benefits associated with manufacturing. Britain seemed to be no nearer to the end of its resources in the 1820s; in fact Malthus began to be worried by the ease with which she made good the ravages of war through capital accumulation. He also accorded greater recognition to the fact that standards of living depended as much on the conveniences and comforts which were increasingly available to the lower classes as on cheaper food. Indeed, he added yet another twist to the luxury debate by claiming that its benefits were greater precisely when luxuries were consumed by the mass of society. His reasons for believing this were connected with a realization that the availability of such goods had permanently beneficial effects on the habits of the populace at large; they were a powerful stimulus to both industry and prudence, and therefore helped to create, along with education, and civil and political liberty, the conditions for *embourgeoisement*.

As on the question of population, therefore, Malthus had come a long way from the pessimistic conclusions of 1798. From a starting position that involved being unfriendly to manufacturing occupations on moral and economic grounds, he gradually accepted that they could bring permanent benefits.

The Corn Laws

No reader of the above arguments on agriculture and manufacturing in the *Essay* should have been surprised when Malthus came out in favour of the retention of that measure of protection conferred by existing Corn Laws in 1814–15. He made his first contribution to public debate in a pamphlet entitled *Observations on the Effects of the Corn Laws, and of a Rise or Fall in the Price of Corn on the Agriculture and General Wealth of the Country* in 1814; and in this work he rehearsed the arguments for and against the Corn Laws in a spirit of 'strictest impartiality'. Despite this, he was regarded by free-traders as having weakened the barriers against error and prejudice. By this time the issue had become a far more divisive one, for not only was there a presumption, which Malthus shared, that 'artificial' systems of bounties and restrictions ran counter to the principles of political economy, but a large body of public opinion had come to regard protection as involving a sacrifice of public interest (especially that of manufacturers, wage-earners, and consumers) to special interests—chiefly those of a landowning aristocracy that also happened to enjoy legislative privileges. Hence both Malthus's courage and moderation in arguing as he did: pamphlet contributions to public debate carried more risk than expressing similar views in a scientific treatise.

As in the *Essay*, Malthus had to counter Smith's authority on the subject by arguing that bounties and restrictions could increase and actually had increased production by raising agricultural prices and profits. At the same time he had to expose fallacies in the case put forward by supporters of the Corn Laws, by employing more orthodox reasoning to show that free trade possessed 'striking advantages' and, consequently, that protection (even maintaining an existing system rather than creating it anew) involved 'sacrifices' (P 124).

Malthus made two more contributions to the debate in the following year; the first, an *Inquiry into the Nature and Progress of Rent*, was an indirect contribution, more scientific in tone and purpose, while the second, *Grounds of an Opinion on the Policy of Restricting the Importation of Foreign Corn*, was intended for more popular consumption. They revealed that Malthus was now a more whole-hearted supporter of the case for retaining protection, and they opened up a rift between him and his Whig and radical friends, especially those responsible for the *Edinburgh Review* and other orthodox devotees of political economy, most notably his friend Ricardo and his two lieutenants, James Mill and J. R. McCulloch. From this moment on Malthus was denied the pages of the *Edinburgh Review* as an outlet for his views on any subject apart from population; he also became the object of hostility from within the political economists' camp, especially from McCulloch and the young John Stuart Mill. This meant that he had to make use of the pages of the *Quarterly Review*, a Tory periodical that had attacked his population views earlier, and that his version of political economy became suspect, incapable of being made the basis for various popular versions of the subject that were appearing at that time, the most significant being the articles on political economy topics in the supplement to the *Encyclopaedia Britannica*.

The new factors which had brought Malthus down from the fence were: evidence of the extent of new investment in agricultural improvement that was likely to be thrown out of employment by any sudden fall in corn prices; the risk of adding to the deflationary effect resulting from a further increase in the value of money; and his belief that such foreign suppliers as France, who now possessed, or so Malthus believed, a permanent cost advantage in grain products, would restrict the export of corn when domestic scarcity threatened. Free-trade principles had to give way in the light of knowledge concerning the quantitative impact of changes in legislation, as well as in the face of the realities of other nations' likely policies.

Malthus's new position emphasized the beneficial effect on wage-earners' living standards of maintaining a high and steady price for food, a case that ran directly counter to the normal argument in favour of cheap foodstuffs. The case required him to maintain that as long as the general demand for labour (and hence levels of employment) remained buoyant, and once money wages were adjusted to the higher corn price, the wage-earner would be able to exert greater command over the non-agricultural 'conveniences and luxuries of life'. Apart from the intrinsic gains involved, Malthus also believed that a combination of high wages and corn prices was more likely to act as a restraint on population growth than low wages and cheap corn. The chief gainers from free trade would be those capitalists who were engaged in foreign trade; but against the possible expansion in demand for British goods abroad associated with free trade had to be set the likelihood of an even larger decline in home demand and employment associated with the fall in agricultural incomes resulting from the influx of foreign corn and declining corn prices.

It was in this context that Malthus introduced his argument for placing a high priority on the 'unproductive' consumption out of rental incomes accruing to landowners. By stressing this source of demand, and by comparing it favourably with that associated with a small minority of stockholders in receipt of incomes from interest on the national debt who might benefit from a fall in the general price level, Malthus upheld, via a different route, a conclusion with which Smith would have agreed, namely that though landowners 'do not so actively contribute to the production of wealth' as other classes, their 'interests are more nearly and intimately connected with the prosperity of the state' (P 162).

Malthus's second pamphlet, though still cautiously argued, conveyed (to free-traders at least) an air of proving too much, both with respect to the benefits to wage-earners and, more especially, with regard to the long-term hopes for food prices. The law of diminishing returns, or the idea that 'in every rich and improving country there is a natural and strong tendency to a constantly increasing price of raw produce, owing to the necessity of employing, progressively, land of an inferior quality', (P 152) provided the basis for the theory of rent which he advanced in *An Inquiry into the Nature and Progress of Rent*. Nevertheless, in *Grounds of an Opinion* Malthus allowed himself to speculate about the possibility of a fall in the price of domestically produced food as a result of improvements in technology.

Rent

The public interest in the Corn Law question had provided Malthus with an excuse for publishing his views on the nature of rent—a subject left in an ambivalent state by Smith, and one on which Malthus had formed a distinctive and original position of his own in the course of his teaching duties. Malthus defined rent as the return to landowners after other costs of production had been met, which meant that the proximate cause of rent was the excess of food prices over costs of production. In some parts of the *Wealth of Nations* Smith had adopted this view, but had also treated it as a kind of monopoly return to the owners of a scarce resource. Malthus was opposed to such an interpretation, especially when it was espoused and elaborated by other writers such as Jean-Baptiste Say, Sismondi, and David Buchanan. To the last of these writers, for instance, the clear implication was that the return to monopoly was at the expense of the consumer; and that rent could therefore be considered as a kind of transfer payment from one class of income recipient to another.

Malthus agreed that there were affinities with natural monopoly based on the limited supply of fertile land available. This justified the term 'partial monopoly', but it was not the end of the story. Another reason for the price of food being above costs was what Malthus sometimes called 'the bounty of Nature', or 'the bountiful gift of Providence'. Land yielded more to labour than was necessary to support those working on land. It was the

source of all power and enjoyment; and without which, in fact there would be no cities, no military or naval force, no arts, no learning, none of the finer manufactures, none of the conveniences and luxuries of foreign countries, and none of that cultivated and polished society, which not only elevates and dignifies individuals, but which extends its beneficial influence through the whole mass of the people. (P 191)

Moreover, the peculiar feature of the necessaries of life was that their supply created demand—another way of expressing the population principle. In other truly natural monopolies demand was 'exterior to, and independent of, the production itself', (P 189) but in the case of food, as opposed, say, to rare wines, 'the demand is dependent upon the produce itself'. As labour and capital became cheaper in the process of growth, so the pressure on land and hence the price paid for its use became greater. What was *originally* a gift came at a higher and higher price to those who arrived late in the Garden of Eden, but it was still a gift because it took the form of surplus. Rent, therefore, was a creature of progress, and would arise whenever a nation attained to any considerable size of population or accumulation. The rent level was a kind of barometer of progress to Malthus, as others had chosen to treat the rate of interest earlier, and Ricardo was to treat profits later. Rising rents were simply the other side of a coin on which accumulation of capital, rising population, extension of cultivation, and a rising price for raw produce were written. It followed that any attempt to bring down the price of produce in order to reduce rent would be accompanied by a withdrawal of cultivation from all but the very best of lands, a movement back along the scale of progress.

In this way Malthus proved that 'the actual state of the natural rent of land is necessary to the actual produce'. The price of food at any given time was equal to the cost of producing it on the least good land. It followed that 'the very circumstance of which we complain, may be the necessary consequence and the most certain sign of increasing wealth and prosperity' (P 209). Nor should we complain on behalf of those most affected by high food prices. The essentials to their well-being were to be found in a combination of prudential habits with regard to marriage and an expanding demand for labour: 'And I do not scruple distinctly to affirm, that under similar habits, and a similar demand for labour, the high price of corn, when it has had time to produce its natural effects, so far from being a disadvantage to them is a positive and unquestionable advantage' (P 215).

The episode reveals a remarkable degree of convergence among political economists upon a theory of rent that was the simultaneous discovery of several authors. Apart from Malthus, Edward West, Robert Torrens, David Buchanan, and Ricardo all reached similar conclusions on the nature and causes of rent based on the law of diminishing returns to marginal land and capital. Nevertheless, in the case of Malthus and Ricardo especially, differing structures were eventually to be erected on the same foundations, which explains not merely the different conclusions which they came to on the subject of the Corn Laws, but, as we shall see in the next chapter, their differences on a wide range of other questions as well. Since the Ricardian alternative against which Malthus found himself increasingly having to argue also originated during the Corn Law debates, it may be helpful at this stage to look at its outlines.

Ricardo's contribution to the Corn Law controversy, his *Essay on the Influence of a Low Price of Corn on the Profits of Stock* (1815), was in part a reply to Malthus, and it was to become the basis for remoulding the shape of political economy which he undertook two years later in his *Principles of Political Economy*. According to Ricardo's view of things, profits throughout the economy were determined by those received by the farmer working on the least fertile land where no rent could be earned. It followed from this that if Britain relied on domestic agriculture to support a growing population, diminishing returns would raise rents and reduce profits, the main motive and source of capital accumulation, thereby impeding future growth. Ricardo's theory also underlined the divisive conclusion of such authors as Buchanan by suggesting that 'the interest of the landlord is always opposed to the interest of every other class in the community' (R IV 21). Anything that raised the price of food, whether it was increasing population, agricultural protection, or poor agricultural methods, increased the share going to the receivers of rents. There could be no more decisive break with the common assumption of eighteenth-century writers, including Smith, that the interest of landowners was always at one with that of the nation under progressive conditions.

Ricardo's answer to Malthus's fears concerning dependence on foreign suppliers was that a stable policy of import would create a reliable British market for foreign suppliers, and that this would lower the price of imported corn. Fluctuations in prices would also be lessened by recourse to a variety of sources, not likely to be moving in the same direction at the same time. Ricardo was proposing what to a large extent happened in Britain later in the century, namely that she should specialize in manufactured goods and rely on her exports of such goods to pay for cheap imports of food and raw materials. Britain's capital would be employed where the return was greatest, a principle of free trade or natural liberty which had been established by Smith under different circumstances. It follows that Ricardo could not share Malthus's anxieties about unbalanced growth.

Hence too Ricardo's difficulty in understanding why Malthus bemoaned the loss of capital involved in any shift away from domestic agriculture. 'We might just as fairly have been told, when the steam-engine, or Mr. Arkwright's cotton-machine, was brought to perfection, that it would be wrong to adopt the use of them, because the value of the old clumsy machinery would be lost to us.' There would be losers in abolishing the Corn Laws, especially those farming on the less fertile land, 'but the public would gain many times the amount of their losses; and, after the exchange of capital from land to manufactures had been effected, the farmers themselves, as well as every other class of the community, except the landholders, would very considerably increase their profits' (R IV 33). Notice also that Ricardo's interpretation of the rent doctrine opened up another rift, namely between capitalist farmers and their landlords.

How could Malthus answer such a persuasive case, one built on principles that he himself upheld on general grounds? One answer was implicit in all his earlier writings, namely that legislative wisdom lay in forsaking wealth whenever the cost in terms of 'happiness' and 'virtue' were found to be excessive. He continued to maintain this position, but he obviously felt the need to provide stronger arguments from within political economy itself, rather than rely on exceptions of a political and moral kind. The germs of his reply can be found in his argument that higher food prices could be advantageous to wage-earners. On this Malthus could rely on his population doctrines: a high price was more likely to curb population growth. But in order to provide an accurate account of all the consequences involved, Malthus also needed to find an alternative answer to Ricardo's belief in the natural equilibrating effects on income and employment levels of markets operating under freely competitive conditions. This eventually entailed a reconsideration of the effect of different policies on the distribution of income, and hence on the level of effective demand, the subject of the next chapter.

It may also be worth pointing out, in conclusion, that while Malthus was, so to speak, on the winning side in 1815—a protective Corn Law was passed, though not necessarily for the reasons given by Malthus—he was not entirely happy with the result. A familiar pattern of popular unrest accompanied the passage of the Bill, and these events clearly shook the moderate politician in Malthus so much that he concluded that the people should not have a divisive measure imposed upon them. Again, the conclusions of his science of politics took precedence over his principles of political economy, but it was characteristic of Malthus that he continued to suffer agonies of conscience throughout his life for the part he may have played in undermining the general principle of non-intervention to which he was deeply attached.

6 The political economy of stable growth

A long and fairly tortuous story precedes the publication of both editions of Malthus's *Principles*, and only slight exaggeration is involved in saying that most readers of the work have had almost as much trouble in deciding what kind of book it is as Malthus had in writing it. During the course of his teaching he had compiled a great deal of material embodying commentary and qualifications to the positions developed by Adam Smith in the *Wealth of Nations*. He made several attempts to publish this material, and the *Inquiry into Rent* and the fifth edition of the *Essay* published in 1817 contain some of the distinctive views on political economy which he had developed in the course of his teaching duties. After Ricardo's *Principles* appeared, Malthus redoubled these efforts to put his views before the public. But it was never his intention to compile 'a new systematic treatise', largely because he did not think the time was ripe for such an ambition. Hence in great measure his difficulties in settling on a title for his response to Ricardo; and while he eventually settled on *The Principles of Political Economy considered with a view to their Practical Application*, it might have been better if he had stuck to the idea of tracts or essays, connected disquisitions on disputed matters. Those who were led to expect that 'practical' meant 'policy' found that they had to make an effort to follow a good deal of deductive theorizing, albeit fleshed out, in Malthusian fashion, with broad historical and empirical material.

The same might be said of two shorter works which were written during the last decade of Malthus's life when he was still trying to codify his thoughts: *The Measure of Value Stated* (1823) and *Definitions in Political Economy* (1827). Modern readers who have not developed a taste for economic reasoning may find they still have to make an effort, but it cannot be avoided in any attempt to understand Malthus's preoccupations, and there may be some consolation in the fact that translating Malthus's ideas into the language of modern economics (largely avoided here) would not ease their problem.

The *Principles* was based on Malthus's belief, in contrast to Ricardo, that 'the science of political economy bears a nearer resemblance to the science of morals and politics than to that of mathematics' (Pr 2); his conviction that one of the chief faults of economists lay in their 'precipitate attempt to simplify and generalize' (Pr 6)—their unwillingness to recognize the multi-causal influences at work in the world and to modify principles in the light of evidence that had accumulated during the half-century that had elapsed since Smith's work first appeared. Once again we see Malthus the moderate at work, attempting to curb 'premature generalisations' by subjecting them to the test of experience, and by constantly stressing the lessons of the doctrine of proportions. In this respect there are similarities between his attitude to Ricardo's doctrines and his attack on Godwin and Condorcet in the first *Essay*. For as he said in a concluding peroration to the *Principles*, although 'we cannot make a science more certain by our wishes or opinions', it was possible to 'make it much more uncertain in its application, by believing it to be what it is not' (Pr 515).

It should now be clear that from the outset of his career as a political economist Malthus was prepared to question the un-qualified application to policy of any single system or principle, however distinguished its lineage, and regardless—as in the case of the population principle—of whether he had formulated it himself. Hence the frequent charges of inconsistency brought against him by fellow-economists. Moreover, if general allegiance to the system of natural liberty, as interpreted by Smith and upheld under the different circumstances by some of his followers, is the hallmark of an orthodox political economist during the first half of the nineteenth century, Malthus occupies a decidedly ambivalent position.

As the opponent of Godwin and others who proposed wholesale departures from a society based on private property and employing competition and self-interest as its chief guiding principles, Malthus was anxious to demonstrate that this form of society was the only one capable of providing the incentives that would guarantee a surplus over basic needs and make rising standards of living possible; that it led to the best available solution by preventing production from going beyond what was economically sustainable, even when this solution fell short of the maximum level of output that was physically possible. This was more than an argument against the feasibility of egalitarian and communitarian schemes of reformation: China and other countries in which population had been 'forced' up to the physical limits of their natural resources served as dire warnings of what could happen if these propositions were ignored.

On the other hand, no other orthodox classical economist pursued quite so many lines of inquiry based on the notion that, for a variety of reasons, economic systems operating under competitive market conditions were not likely to be self-adjusting—or, what amounts to the same thing, capable of adjusting in ways and over time-periods that were acceptable on economic or moral grounds. It was this concern with what happens in the process of adjusting from one constellation of economic forces to another which lends a consistently dynamic dimension to Malthus's work as a political economist. Nor did any other contemporary economist of similar prominence lay so much emphasis on the limits to stable growth arising from the failure of effective demand to expand in harmony with an economy's aggregate supply or capacity to produce. Although Malthus's proposals for institutional change and state intervention to overcome these problems

77

of maladjustment, whether of a temporary or more deep-seated variety, were fairly tentative (his opponents described them as hesitant and vacillating), the underlying preoccupations cannot be ignored in any attempt to understand his method of approach and choice of questions that needed to be answered. Malthus's political economy manifested a persistent concern with fluctuations, instability, limits to growth, possible sources of stagnation, and ways in which the plans and expectations of individuals and groups of economic actors could be frustrated or left unfulfilled in ways that imperilled the continuity of economic life.

Cycles

The earliest signs of this interest are to be found in the treatment given to 'perpetual oscillation' in the first *Essay*—to the cycles, perhaps of some sixteen to eighteen years' duration, which arose from the delayed response of population to the rise or fall in real wages. This helped to explain periodic over-supply, unemployment, and general distress. Ricardo put his finger on a major difference between himself and Malthus when he observed that Malthus always had in mind 'the immediate and temporary effects of particular changes', while he concentrated on the 'permanent state of things which will result from them' (R VII 120). In agreeing with this observation, while noting implicitly that 'temporary effects' might not be confined to a few months or even years, Malthus defended his priorities by saying that: 'I really think that the progress of society consists of irregular movements, and that to omit the consideration of causes which for eight or ten years will give a great *stimulus* to production and population, or a great *check* to them, is to omit the causes of the wealth and poverty of nations—the grand object of all enquiries in Political Economy' (R VII 122). The final paragraph of the *Principles* shows the same concern, with Malthus complaining that 'theoretical writers' (which usually means Ricardo and his followers) have overlooked the consequences, judged by utilitarian standards, of these 'serious spaces in human life':

They amount to a serious sum of happiness or misery, according as they are prosperous or adverse, and leave the country in a very different state at their termination. In prosperous times the mercantile classes often realize fortunes which go far towards securing them against the future; but unfortunately the working classes, though they share in the general prosperity, do not share so largely as in the general adversity. They may suffer the greatest distress in a period of low wages, but cannot be adequately compensated by a period of high wages. To them fluctuations must alway bring more evil than good; and, with a view to the happiness of the great mass of society, it should be our object, as far as possible, to maintain peace, and an equable expenditure. (Pr 522)

The reference here to peace signals the connection with the prolonged period of economic distress that followed the cessation of hostilities in 1815. In seeking explanations for this phenomenon—a topic they were still actively debating in the 1820s—Malthus and Ricardo revealed all their main differences on matters of theory and policy. For it was when advancing his diagnosis and remedies for post-war depression that Malthus further developed the principle of 'effective or effectual demand'. We have noted his use of this principle in various arguments put forward in the later revisions to the *Essay* and in his Corn Law pamphlets—arguments to the effect that when the demand for labour was expanding it was possible for the poor to be rich in the midst of general dearness. This was a precondition for his belief that a combination of high food prices and wages was beneficial to wage-earners. The 1817 edition of the *Essay* also enabled Malthus to incorporate his diagnosis of post-war depression: the conditions most conducive to improvements in the condition of wage-earners, a buoyant effective demand for the products of labour, yielded, by inversion, an explanation for what had gone wrong after the war.

According to Malthus the post-war depression was triggered by the fall in corn prices after exceptionally good harvests in

1814–15. The resulting fall in the incomes of landowners and farmers, accompanied by a failure of money wages to fall in line with food prices, had led to a reduction in agricultural employment and a fall in the home demand for manufactured goods. This in turn had led to export markets being over-supplied and a consequent decline in mercantile incomes. The extent of the depression was partly connected with the immense stimulus given to population and production during the war, and partly with special factors connected with demobilization of the military, high taxes and national debt, and a decline in the general price level due to a reduction in the money supply. Here was a situation in which rents, profits, wages, and prices were simultaneously depressed, and redundant capital was being driven to find employment abroad.

Malthus felt that this evidence was incompatible with two of Ricardo's leading doctrines: his explanation for profit decline in terms of higher wages resulting from diminishing returns in agriculture (a limiting but not a determining condition in Malthus's view): and his diagnosis of the depression as one involving partial rather than general glut. The latter position relied on a proposition associated with the names of Jean-Baptiste Say and James Mill to the effect that aggregate supply or output was always capable of generating a level of aggregate demand that would ensure the sale of all goods produced. According to this proposition, while the markets for some goods could be overstocked, an equivalent understocking would be taking place elsewhere—an idea which Malthus thought was comparable to the assertion 'that every man in the streets of London who was observed to have his head covered, would be found upon examination to have his feet bare' (Q 204).

Whereas Ricardo treated post-war depression and unemployment as a problem of maladjustment due to a mismatch in the demand and supply of individual commodities, Malthus regarded it as evidence of a general deficiency of demand in relation to supply, leading to all markets being overstocked and profits being depressed across the board. Ricardo's solution was to restore prosperity by encouraging investment, chiefly through a reduction in taxes and the burden of national debt, and by allowing market forces to bring about a realignment of the detailed pattern of demand and supply. Although Malthus agreed that cycles had self-correcting features, he also felt that the war stimulus, followed by a severe post-war check to prosperity, had unusual features which warranted special ameliorative action. He was opposed to Ricardo's idea that what was needed, above all, was an increase in capital accumulation under circumstances in which it was manifest that profits and trade were generally depressed.

In order to clarify his position on this point Malthus drew parallels between periods of redundant population and redundant capital. Each was subject to cycles arising from an over-response to earlier conditions of high wages and profits. And just as there were limits to the rate of increase in population which could be sustained without damaging living standards, so there were limits to the volume of savings that could be invested with any hope of obtaining a return that would cover costs and give an adequate incentive to continue production: 'it is equally vain, with a view to the permanent increase of wealth, to continue converting revenue into capital, when there is no adequate demand for the products of such capital, as to continue encouraging marriage and the birth of children without a demand for labour and an increase of the funds for its maintenance' (Pr 375).

The population parallel also consorted well with Malthus's attitude to short-term remedies. For just as the Poor Law and other emergency measures could be justified during exceptional periods of rising food prices, so short-term measures were warranted in order to bring the economy through a cyclical downturn involving an excess of productive potential over effective demand. Addressing himself specifically to the peculiarities of the post-war period, Malthus was not in favour of any sharp reduction of taxes, retirement of debt, and further cuts in public expenditure. This would increase the risk of reducing effective demand in conditions where the productive potential of the economy had been greatly increased during the war. He advocated caution in the removal of protective duties on goods that were competitive with the products of domestic industries, and was anxious to find ways of affording relief to the un-employed by encouraging those capable of increasing the demand for 'unproductive labour' to do so. These could either be 'land-lords and persons of property' who might be induced 'to build, to improve and beautify their grounds, and to employ workmen and menial servants'; or relief might take the form of activities, 'the results of which do not come for sale into the market, such as roads and public works' (Pr 511). Such diversions of expenditure away from productive employments, though not justifiable under conditions of full employment, were 'exactly what is wanted' as a counter-balancing factor when there was 'a failure of the national demand for labour' connected with a sudden shift, under con-ditions of general glut, from the unproductive labour of war towards productive employment. Contrary to the views of some pro-inflationist writers, however, Malthus was not in favour of increasing the quantity of money as a means of raising prices on grounds of the temporary nature of the stimulus and the secondary role played by money in the process of wealth expansion and contraction.

On all these matters Malthus found himself in stark conflict with Ricardo's thinking. An increase in expenditure on un-productive labour, Ricardo commented, was 'just as necessary and as useful with a view to future production, as a fire, which should consume in the manufacturer's warehouse the goods which those unproductive labourers would otherwise consume' (R II 421). And as for public expenditure: 'What could be more wise if Mr. Malthus doctrine be true than to increase the army, and double the salaries of all the officers of Government?' (R II

450). Malthus did not reply to these jibes directly in the second edition of the *Principles*, one reason being that in the context of depression produced by a general over-supply of commodities, consumption meant for him exactly what Ricardo was ridiculing, namely 'used up' or consumed as in a fire. Similarly, while Malthus would not have approved of an increase in the wages or salaries of those employed by public funds as a remedy for depression, he was in favour of increasing public employment in fields that did not add to the existing excess supply of goods. Since Ricardo and all those who adopted the Say–Mill view of things denied the possibility of general glut, it is no wonder that they were bemused by Malthus's heterodox solutions to what they regarded as a non-existent problem.

Effective demand and stable growth

Sharp though these disagreements over both diagnosis and remedies for post-war depression were, they were largely by-products of an issue which is more central to Malthus's *Principles*, namely the discovery of 'the most immediate and effective stimulants to the continued creation and progress of wealth'. This interest in long-run growth prospects, in those institutional and other factors which explained progressive, stationary, and retro-grade states of society, was also present in the treatment given to agricultural, manufacturing, and mixed states in the *Essay*. But Malthus gave the theme greater unity and prominence in the *Principles* by focusing on effective demand as one of the essential guarantors of stable and sustainable growth. The significance and peculiarity of Malthus's position on unproductive labour and consumption is also more readily appreciable when placed within the context of these long-run concerns.

Here too Malthus found himself in conflict with the implications of the Say–Mill Law of Markets, as it has come to be called, namely that if capital accumulation and the aggregate

83

supply of goods were increasing over time, the appropriate level of aggregate demand would follow in its train. Once goods had been produced, both the power and the will to consume them existed; economic growth and full employment were entirely compatible. Ricardo's model envisaged, as a theoretical possibility at least, the existence of a 'stationary state' at which profits would be reduced by rising food costs and wages to a level at which there would be no further incentive to invest—a state in which all further growth would cease. But he was anxious to deny that this condition was near at hand, or had actually been reached by Britain, and that it entailed any breakdown in market processes. He was especially anxious to deny any suggestion that the prolonged conditions of post-war depression heralded the arrival of 'a retrograde state of society'. Once the economy had adjusted to post-war conditions, once taxes and the burden of debt had been reduced, and certain unwise policies such as agricultural protection had been abandoned, Ricardo believed that Britain enjoyed almost unlimited scope for further investment and growth.

It is not difficult to see how an argument about partial as opposed to general gluts could become confused with another one involving the distinction between temporary and permanent stagnation. On the surface at least, post-war depression lent support to both positions. The evidence immediately available did not allow a distinction to be made between a situation that was partial and temporary, and one that was general and presaged a permanent retardation. Neither Ricardo nor Malthus succeeded in keeping the problems of short-term cycles and long-term growth prospects separate. There are signs too that Malthus believed—when writing during the post-war period slump at least—that cyclical depression might have more permanent effects. But in order to understand the nature of Malthus's challenge it is helpful to treat the short-term cycle as an acute or special (rather than a chronic or generic) case of principles he had worked out to deal with long-run problems. He was not so much contesting Ricardo's basic optimism about Britain's growth prospects as drawing attention to an important set of pre-conditions for stable growth that played no part in Ricardo's account. Malthus's main divergence centred on whether the progress or retardation of wealth could be understood simply in terms of the physical factors underlying the productive potential or aggregate supply side of the economy—its labour force, capital stock, and command over natural resources and technology. To this needed to be added, he believed, an account of the variables which determined the level of effective demand, where the main connections between aggregate supply and demand could be found in a distribution of income and expenditure that favoured continued growth.

The problem was largely one of how to sustain economic motivation, a problem which Malthus regarded as being crucial and constant, not merely in poor and what would later be called underdeveloped economies, but in countries like Britain as well. This was a reflection of assumptions about the constancy of human nature that were displayed in the first *Essay* when arguing for the Newtonian character of the social world. It featured in his debate with Ricardo as a question of whether the existence of the *power* to produce and consume guaranteed that the *will* to produce and consume would automatically follow, and if not, what kind of stimulants were needed to make it do so. Whereas Ricardo held that 'will is very seldom wanting when the power exists', Malthus maintained that the inertial forces of 'indolence' were ever-present and had to be overcome by new stimuli, new wants, and new incentives to acquire additional wealth. Ricardo and Malthus were agreed that in theory wants were insatiable; the question at issue was whether, and under what circumstances, the main actors in the economic drama would be prepared to make the necessary sacrifices in terms of leisure foregone in order to obtain the additional goods that would satisfy these wants; whether, in the terminology Malthus employed, luxuries would always be preferred to indolence. Ricardo found such concerns otiose; they might explain slow growth or stagnation in the past, and in China, Latin America, and Ireland in the present, but they were irrelevant to a country like Britain 'with a dense population abounding in capital, skill, commerce, and manufacturing industry, and with tastes for every enjoyment that nature, art or science will procure' (R II 340).

Malthus's answer to this and other questions can be found in a long chapter 'On the Immediate Causes of the Progress of Wealth', which first reviews the factors which underlie the power to produce—population, capital accumulation, fertility of the soil, and 'inventions to abridge labour'—in order to show that, in themselves, acting separately or in combination, they were incapable of generating sustained growth. The missing element was effective demand, which in turn depended on the way in which the total product of society was distributed between the different economic classes, and on whether production was adapted to the wants of consumers. The conditions for effective demand were satisfied when a level of prices existed that was capable of covering all production costs and of giving a return on capital sufficient to serve as an incentive to continue production.

The concept of effective demand rested on the distinction between productive and unproductive consumption which we have already encountered when dealing with Malthus's diagnosis of the post-war depression. Capital accumulation entailed the use of revenue or income for purposes of productive consumption. Although it referred to a form of expenditure on material goods, and was not, therefore, the exclusive province of any class of income recipient, much of the discussion between Malthus and Ricardo was conducted on the assumption that capital accumulation was chiefly an activity or propensity associated with capitalists, those in receipt of profits as opposed to rents and wages. It involved the translation of savings into investment in order to employ labour with a view to producing further profit from the sale of material goods. Unproductive consumption entailed either the purchase of labour services as an end in itself, or the production of material goods that were not intended for sale on the market. The former activity was usually taken to be the main propensity of landowners or rent-receivers, with those in receipt of interest from their holdings of public debt being added, particularly after a war in which such holdings had grown considerably. Again though, it was the nature of the expenditure rather than the form of income from which it derived that mattered most. Although unproductive consumption did not create wealth, it was, according to Malthus, an essential ingredient on the demand side acting as a stimulus to wealth-creation. Maintaining the correct balance between these two activities, therefore, contained the clue to a healthy state of effective demand. It explains Malthus's unorthodox belief, hinted at in his criticisms of Smith in the first *Essay* and developed in opposition to Ricardo in the *Principles*, that 'the principle of saving, pushed to excess, would destroy the motive to production' (Pr 8). While investment of the savings of capitalists (productive consumption) undoubtedly increased the demand of those who were in receipt of wages from such employment, this needed to be supplemented by unproductive consumption to ensure that the increase in output associated with investment was purchased at prices capable of covering the costs of production. If this condition was not met, Malthus believed that the expectations of all savers/investors could be frustrated: there would be insufficient demand to ensure that profits were realized and that production at the new, higher levels would continue. If the doctrine of proportions was not observed in this matter, growth could be impeded rather than facilitated by increased saving/investment.

When Malthus diagnosed an excess of aggregate supply over demand, resulting in a level of output that could not be sold at cost-covering prices, he naturally thought of repairing the deficiency by increasing the level of unproductive consumption by those in receipt of rental and *rentier* incomes. Rents were particularly suitable for this purpose, being earned as a result of the contribution of a natural resource to production, but not for any specific contribution which the ownership of land made to output. Similarly with some public works; they generated incomes and employment without increasing the supply of goods to what might be an overstocked market in which prices and profits were already depressed.

In upholding this position, Malthus has been treated, as he was by Ricardo and his followers, as committing a version of a common 'underconsumptionist' fallacy—the fallacy of believing that, under circumstances which could be either temporary or permanent, the conversion of savings into investment might not be matched by a sufficient volume of demand, either for goods or services, to ensure continued success. The employment of wage-earners resulting from additional investment, though a positive contribution to aggregate demand, might need to be supplemented from other sources to achieve balance. Malthus did not treat saving as 'hoarding' (an increase in idle money balances and hence a subtraction from the income flow), and he endorsed Smith's conclusion that 'the produce which is annually saved is as regularly consumed as that which is annually spent, but that it is consumed by a different set of people'—a concession which Ricardo regarded as being at odds with everything else Malthus wished to contend on this subject. The answer to the apparent contradiction seems to be that Malthus was not raising doubts about unrequited leakages from the annual circular flow, so much as pointing to the fact that an economy in which productive capacity was growing would need ever-higher levels of aggregate demand to secure full employment. This was not a simple matter of fallacious reasoning; rather it was a case of adopting a more pessimistic or cautious view of the opportunities for expanding effective demand sufficiently over time. Malthus's position clearly made sense during the post-war depression, but, with the benefit of hindsight at least, Ricardo's more robust attitude to the ease with which new wants could be released has more to be said for it over the longer period. In recommending that under some circumstances it might be necessary to practice a form of moral restraint with regard to investment, Malthus seems, once more, to be cast in the role of a Cassandra proved wrong by subsequent developments.

Yet this cannot be the last word on the subject, any more than it would be correct to think of Malthus as entertaining dismal views on the impossibility of ever achieving a combination of rising population and living standards. First one must bear in mind the size of the historical and geographical canvas on which Malthus painted. As a historical analysis of the barriers to economic growth in the European past, and as a diagnosis of the difficulties that had to be overcome in Africa, Asia, and Latin America, Malthus's approach, as Ricardo conceded, had a great deal to commend it. It amounted to saying that, in addition to some essential institutional requirements connected with security of property and political stability, a steady expansion of demand, bringing with it rising prices and profits, was a major pre-condition for sustainable growth. In this respect Malthus remained closer to Hume and Smith in paying more attention to political and moral variables affecting economic habits, and to expansive forces connected with wider markets and the spread of market incentives.

This becomes obvious when Malthus turns to consider those ways in which the distribution of incomes arising from economic activity affect economic growth, favourably or otherwise. The treatment given to this subject is basically a re-examination of some of the topics Smith had dealt with when describing the causes and consequences of the breakup of feudalism, and when illustrating his proposition that the division of labour, and hence the productive powers of society, were dependent on ever-wider extensions of the market.

Malthus's account is organized under three main headings; the division of landed property; the spread of internal and external commerce; and the maintenance of a body of unproductive consumers. Only on the last of these does Malthus depart from Smithian premisses. The 'unequal and vicious' division of land under feudalism, creating a small number of wealthy consumers and a large body of poor producers, was highly unfavourable to effective demand, to incentives, and to the adoption of improved methods of production. The subdivision of land, by creating a larger number of smaller consumers and producers, had been an essential step towards making continuous growth possible. This was the solution which Malthus had recommended in the later editions of the *Essay* to the problems of such countries as Russia and Poland. The doctrine of proportions, however, suggested that this process could be carried too far. Thus, Malthus was not in favour of Britain following the French example in abolishing primogeniture, which could lead to a peasantry living at bare subsistence levels and vulnerable both to food shortage and 'military despotism' (Pr 434). Economic and political considerations could not be separated in a matter of this importance.

Primogeniture had swelled the ranks of effective demanders by forcing younger sons (like himself, it might be added) to seek incomes from commerce, manufacturing, the professions, and from dividends on private shares and public debt. What was referred to earlier as Malthus's 'Country' Whig allegiances have a role to play here in disposing him to believe that English liberties depended on the continued existence of a landed aristocracy. But it is a sign of the direction in which his thoughts were moving that in the second edition of the *Principles* he added the middle classes as guardians of liberty when endorsing the benefits of the Reform Bill of 1832 in extending the franchise. He also welcomed the likely further effect of an increase in the size of the manufacturing and commercial sector in generating greater equality, and he attempted to neutralize the connotations of his discussion of unproductive labour by referring instead to a demand for 'personal services'. Landowners, and an 'idle' *rentier* class generally, were no longer the sole source of what Ricardo thought of simply as wasteful expenditure. The demand for any kind of services that generated employment would increasingly come from a wide variety of sources of income.

The expansion of markets through improved internal and external communications has a more obvious basis in Smith's views on extension of the market and the division of labour. The only novelty in Malthus's discussion of this factor lies in his attempt to combat Ricardo's more restricted account of the gains from trade based on his theory of profits. Whereas Ricardo felt that the chief gain would come through a reduction of wages as a result of the importation of cheaper grain products and a consequential rise in profits, Malthus adhered to Smith's more common-sense view that anything which increased the foreign demand for domestic products would raise both wages and profits. With regard to imports, Malthus stressed their 'tendency to inspire new wants, to form new tastes, and to furnish fresh motives for industry', a species of gain which was not of a once-and-for-all variety, and consequently one which 'even civilized and improved countries cannot afford to lose' (Pr 470).

In this case, therefore, Malthus might be said to have adopted a more dynamic, and possibly a more optimistic, view of foreign trade than Ricardo. The same is true of his views on the introduction of machinery, a subject on which Ricardo had dismayed his followers by withdrawing his original opinion that machinery always benefited wage-earners. Given Malthus's belief, expressed as early as 1798, that 'the invention of processes for shortening labour without the proportional extension of the market for the commodity' (FE 34) could be damaging, he might have been expected to follow Ricardo's newer, less optimistic position. In fact, however, Malthus stated that Ricardo had gone too far in a pessimistic direction; there were many circumstances in which new machinery cheapened the product, expanded the market, and led to increased employment: the growth of Manchester, for example, testified to the fact that the demand for the products of the Lancashire cotton industry, as cheapened by machinery, had proved to be elastic.

Most of what Malthus has to say on the balance between productive and unproductive consumers, between savers and spenders, the purchasers of material goods and those who bought personal services has been covered earlier. The only observation worth making in conclusion is that to understand Malthus's position it is necessary to bear in mind not merely the post-war depression, but the fact that he was combating a doctrine of Ricardo's to the effect that the *only* limits to further growth were to be found in the difficulties of procuring food. Since the origins of Ricardo's model are to be found in his case for abolishing the Corn Laws, a conclusion resisted by Malthus, an element of polemical exaggeration on this point should perhaps be entered on both sides of the account. Over the whole spectrum of subjects in dispute, however, which included more metaphysical topics such as the measure of value as well as theories of wages, rent, and profits, the differences are more readily attributable to genuine differences of intellectual style and opinion, where again the participants showed considerable awareness of the source of their divergence. Ricardo put the matter thus:

If I am too theoretical, which I really believe is the case, you are too practical. There are so many combinations, so many operating causes in Political Economy, that there is great danger in appealing to experience in favour of a particular doctrine, unless we are sure that all the causes of variation are seen and their effects duly estimated. (R VI 295)

Malthus recognized the inescapable role played by theory and the impossibility of solving complex problems by simple appeals to practical common sense. But he lacked Ricardo's confidence in thinking that economics was 'a strict science like mathematics'

(R VIII 331), and his commitment to experience as the ultimate arbiter was consequently stronger, whatever the result might be in terms of tidiness.

It is not difficult to understand why Keynes, looking back on this dispute from the vantage point of the 1930s, another period of severe depression, found much that was congenial in Malthus (see Chapter 1). But it also seems important to recognize that Malthus's challenge, first to Smith and later to Ricardo, includes, but goes well beyond the kinds of questions which Keynes was to make his own a hundred or so years later. It was not simply that Malthus, like Keynes, was responsive to those 'serious spaces in human life' which may get overlooked in the search for the 'permanent state of things', believing, as Keynes memorably put it, that 'in the long run we are all dead'. Malthus was also concerned about growth prospects over periods of time in which we *are* each likely to be dead.

7 Conclusion

Much of this book has been devoted to answering a deceptively simple historical question: what was Malthus attempting to say to his contemporaries? What, in effect, was he trying to *do* in his various writings on population and political economy? The question of whether he was right in what he contended or did, where 'right' could connote either scientific or moral truth, has been a lesser concern. Yet to those for whom the study of a past thinker must be made subservient to present preoccupations if it is to avoid the sin, harmless or otherwise, of antiquarianism, these priorities may seem perverse, even evasive. What does Malthus have to say that is both new and true to a late twentieth-century audience? That seems a simpler, certainly a blunter way of getting to the heart of matters; and in the case of someone who was self-consciously striving to advance the claims of a science that was capable, in principle at least, of explaining events occurring at all known times and places, it may not only seem to be the most appropriate question, but one that is capable of being answered in a fairly straightforward fashion.

In order to do so, however, one has to begin, in deference to the modern academic division of labour, by distinguishing between Malthus the population theorist and Malthus the political economist, despite the historical fact that the latter role emerged directly from the concerns of the former. One also has to separate Malthus the moralist from Malthus the social scientist, or, more precisely, from Malthus treated as a social scientist according to some influential current interpretations of what a modern social scientist should look like. Having rearranged the intellectual landscape to suit modern tastes, it is then possible to consider Malthus's merits and demerits as a guide to the problems of his own day and ours, praising his pioneering qualities in some cases, but also pointing out the numerous ways in which his formulation of the issues has been improved on, and his predictions falsified—a process which can be carried out with varying degrees of sympathy, often largely depending, in the case of his demographic ideas, on whether the interpreter believes that population pressure in some form is, or is not, a major issue in some part of the world today.

The demographer

As a guide to demographic trends in his own society during the first three decades of the nineteenth century, Malthus has been criticized for paying insufficient attention to the quantitative evidence that was available to him, and for misinterpreting it when he did. His account of the effects on marriage and birth rates of the old Poor Law, the incompleteness of his system of checks as a model for the variables affecting fertility, notably with respect to age-structure and sex-composition, and his assignment of the causes of population growth have all been subject to attacks of this kind. In recent years, however, it has been acknowledged that the connections, or feed-back mechanisms, which he envisaged between food supply and the response of population are more sophisticated than polemical versions of the doctrine suggest. Historical demographers are also willing to grant that he provides a valuable guide to the behaviour of population in pre-industrial societies, thereby adding an element of historical irony to his career: his views were published just as they were about to be made irrelevant, first by the industrial revolution, the discovery of non-land-using raw materials, and the subsequent fall in the price of foodstuffs produced by new suppliers in North America and Australasia, and later by the more widespread use of contraceptive methods. The Malthusian trap was escaped by two exits, one of which he thought was guarded by a tough retaining spring (food supplies), while the other involved the use of methods which he believed to be 'unnatural', immoral, and likely 'to remove a necessary stimulus to industry' (E II 479).

Considered as a predictive device, the dramatic use of the geometric and arithmetic ratios has always given rise to criticism by friends and foes alike. As Malthus himself revealed, the geometric ratio can be reformulated as a fruitful negative hypothesis—why does something *not* happen which an abstract law suggests is possible? The arithmetic ratio is more difficult to rescue, particularly when treated as a *law* of diminishing returns—whatever sense it may have made when interpreted as an inductive inference based on the state of the agricultural arts over a short-run period during the early years of the nineteenth century. But judged in terms of predictions licensed by the crudest form of the Malthusian principle, the whole system has long been exploded. Our capacity to increase food production has been nearer the geometric ratio, and our rate of population increase has been far lower than the maximum posited, though never claimed as an observation, by Malthus. Neither food production nor the supply of natural resources generally, seem capable of acting as a *permanent* constraint on growth rates and living standards. If we contrast the technocratic visions of Godwin and Condorcet with Malthus at his gloomiest, Malthus's opponents appear to have had the last laugh. Whether one appreciates the joke, however, still depends on where one lives in the world, and within which stratum of society.

Some critics have taken the matter further by suggesting that Malthus was guilty of a less venial crime, that of confusing moral and scientific categories, of allowing the former to influence his understanding of the latter, and of propounding a theory that was inherently untestable by virtue of its deductive, even tautological features. They are not impressed by the mass of historical, statistical and ethnographic material which he assembled, or by the fact that towards the end of his life he became a founder-member of the Statistical Section of the British Association for the Advancement of Science and of the London Statistical Society. The material used by Malthus merely becomes, in this light, a set of confirmatory illustrations of propositions which were arrived at by means that have little to do with observation, and, more seriously, were incapable of being subjected to scientific proof or rejection. Thus, when Malthus acknowledged that contemporary evidence did not square with his original prediction that the Poor Laws would encourage early marriage, he concluded that moral restraint must have been more widely practised than he had dared to hope. But instead of being regarded as an example of honesty in the face of facts that ran contrary to one of his predictions, this move is taken to be an attempt to save theoretical appearances by invoking the operation of a moral variable that could not be independently measured. No mitigation of sentence is apparently allowed for the fact that Malthus himself regretted the lack of information that would have allowed him to assign precise weight to the different checks operating singly.

Although such questions could be the essential ones for modern demographers, agronomists, human ecologists, and development specialists, they are certainly not the only ones that can be asked of Malthus. Indeed, it is not clear that they require very much knowledge of Malthus to be answered. They do, however, possess an advantage in their capacity to be framed in fairly precise terms; and in this respect they are less tendentious than those questions which are asked, often on the basis of a presumptively unified twentieth-century morality, about whether Malthus was morally and politically right or wrong in proposing the solutions that he did. As in Malthus's day, this still describes a large body of modern criticism, where the object is basically a recruiting or labelling exercise designed to assign white or black hats to the various historical cowboys.

Given that such questions are suspect or arbitrary, how ought we to look at his work? It has been suggested here that he is best seen as someone committed to the enterprise of constructing and applying a science of politics and morals. This is a reversal of Keynes's description of the trajectory of Malthus's career—'from being a caterpillar of a moral scientist and chrysalis of an historian, he could at last spread the wings of his thought and survey the world as an economist'. Although most economists have understandably been grateful to accept this description, it has been argued here that the population principle and the various ideas on political economy which Malthus advanced were intended more as contributions to the larger and higher scientific vocation of moral scientist. This meant that he was engaged over a wider front than most modern social scientists, including some of his contemporaries. Thus, in Ricardo's eyes Malthus was prone to confuse matters of economic analysis with moral considerations. For example, with regard to rent treated as a gift of a benevolent Creator, Ricardo protested that 'in a treatise on Political Economy it should be so considered. The gift is great or little according as it is more or less, not according as it may be more or less morally useful. It may be better for the health of my friend, that I should restrict him to a pint of wine a day, but my gift is most valuable if I give him a bottle of wine a day' (R II 210). Similarly with Malthus's argument based on the moral advantages of a high price of corn, Ricardo regarded this as an example of failure to recognize that it was the duty of the political economist 'to tell you how you may become rich, but he is not to advise you to prefer riches to indolence, or indolence to riches' (R II 338).

As a guide to individual conduct, Malthus would probably not have disagreed with this proposition; he was not so much preaching individual morality as pointing out the social benefits, largely in terms of stable economic progress, associated with the preference for riches over indolence. He came closer to the preaching role on the subject of moral restraint, though even here he claimed to be taking 'man as he is, with all his imperfections on his head' (E II 463). Preaching morality was secondary to the role of moral scientist capable of elucidating principles, assessing their application to the real world, and attempting to gain support for them. In this, as in so many other respects, he was combining the role of scientist and Christian moralist, and answerable under both rubrics. This distinguishes him from his more secular-minded friends and other political economists who were either without religion or kept it in a separate compartment; but it does not mark him out from other contemporaries who were attempting to create a specifically Christian version of political economy—John Bird Sumner, Richard Jones (his successor at the East India College), Richard Whateley, William Whewell, and Thomas Chalmers. And once a science of morals is understood to be the main point of the exercise, it may be possible to pass a less anachronistic verdict on Malthus's successes and failures. Although social scientists sometimes attempt to measure what Malthus would have regarded as 'moral' variables, and there are, of course, recognizably Christian positions on moral questions, it is rare in the twentieth century to hear anyone speaking of a *science* of morals in the straightforward sense available to Malthus. Whether the relinquishment of such explicit claims represents an advance or not would require another book to answer.

Having brought Malthus's cloth into the reckoning, it is also necessary to confront the uses that have frequently been made of the clerical card. One can either join Marx and Engels in saying that it virtually establishes his credentials as sycophant of the ruling classes, or maintain that the Reverend Malthus was a more humanitarian figure who sometimes came to the rescue of that hard-hearted animal, Population Malthus. With regard to the latter view, there seem to be no good reasons for assuming that Malthus was any more or less humanitarian than anybody else, including his modern critics, and I have given other reasons for doubting the existence of a split personality. As a sincere

Christian, committed both to natural theology and the truths of revealed religion, it was Malthus's duty to engage in apologetics, technically defined, namely to illustrate and explicate the essential wisdom and beneficence of God's design for mankind. But was he an apologist in some more ideological sense entailing the conscious or unconscious defence of established interests from a perspective that could not be justified on grounds of science?

That apologetic uses, in this sense, were made of some of his ideas can hardly be denied. Long before Marx posed the charges in what has become the classic ideological form, Nassau Senior gave this as a reason for being prejudiced against Malthus's population principle: 'I found that principle made the stalking-horse of negligence and injustice, the favourite objection to every project for rendering the resources of the country more productive.' Malthus himself complained that he had been unfortunate in his followers: his doctrines had 'by no means the gloomy aspect given to them by many of my readers'. His speedy withdrawal of the polemical passage in the second *Essay* which suggested that those who came to 'nature's mighty feast' (E 1803 ed. II 531) without the means of paying for their meal had no right to sit at table is an indication of his desire to combat such readings, unavailing though this attempt was. The appendices which he added to the *Essay* in answer to his critics are further proof that he was conscious of the problems of misuse and did his best to overcome them. He also had to face similar charges when he announced his support for the Corn Laws and defended incomes derived from rent, both cases where he was accused of selling out to the landowning interest, and where, by inversion, his opponent Ricardo was thought to have injected a radical and anti-aristocratic political bias into his views.

Was the disagreement between Malthus and Ricardo really one about politics and relative degrees of fondness or antagonism to the landed classes? In explaining their differences over the Corn Laws and rent, perhaps some weight should be allowed to this factor. Malthus's brand of Whig politics did stress the political virtues which attached to the historical role played by the country gentry as the guardians of English liberties, though as his remarks on feudalism and the concentration of landownership show, this should not be confused with an unalloyed belief in the virtues of the landed aristocracy. For his part, Ricardo, who became a follower of the 'philosophic radical' line on the reform of Parliament—a line which relied heavily, particularly in James Mill's hands, on antagonism to the aristocratic principle and the kind of Whig politics which Malthus epitomized—might also seem to have had larger political goals in view. But Ricardo was never as fervent on such matters as his political mentor; he certainly denied animus towards the recipients of rental incomes when it was put to him by Malthus. On the divisive political issue posed by the Corn Laws, Malthus always maintained that the private interests of farmers and landowners, or any other producers' pressure group, were irrelevant to the question of public interest which it was the object of the science of political economy to establish: 'The sole object of our consideration ought to be the permanent interest of the consumer, in the character of which is comprehended the whole nation.' And just as Ricardo defended his friend from charges of political bias, so Malthus took pleasure in pointing out that:

It is somewhat singular that Mr. Ricardo, a considerable receiver of rents, should have so much underrated their national importance; while I, who never received, nor expect to receive any, shall probably be accused of overrating their importance. Our different situations and opinions may serve at least to shew our mutual sincerity, and afford a strong presumption that to whatever bias our minds may have been subjected in the doctrines we have laid down, it has not been that, against which perhaps it is most difficult to guard, the insensible bias of situation and interest. (Pr 222–3)

On the subject of the Poor Laws Malthus stated that: 'If all could be completely relieved, and poverty banished from the

101

country, even at the expense of three-fourths of the fortunes of the rich, I would be the last person to say a single syllable against relieving all, and making the degree of distress alone the measure of our bounty' (E II 369). Neither of these statements, of course, has prevented others, both then and since, from treating him as being insincere or deluded in his protestations.

Judged by later nineteenth-century standards, those of 'self-help' and even the 'survival of the fittest', Malthus has often been seen as having all the necessary qualifications for a full-blown progenitor of a harsh *laissez-faire* position that attributes poverty to weakness of individual character alone. He has certainly been accorded this status by those who place this construction on Darwin's acknowledgements of his indebtedness to Malthus at a crucial stage in the working-out of his theory of natural selection. But, for reasons given in an earlier chapter, the Newtonian in Malthus outweighs the proto-Social Darwinist. However heavily Malthus's God may appear to have loaded the scales in favour of Nature as opposed to Culture, and however much individual prudence was expected to be one of the main agencies for delivering man from its unavoidable evil consequences, Malthus's God was still a Newtonian—meaning that poverty had to be the product of general laws acting on mankind in general rather than visited only on the morally unworthy by a ruthless struggle between individuals or classes. Some of Malthus's poor may be indolent, but they share this characteristic of human nature with the rich. Moreover, just as there is no scope for moral restraint in the natural world, so there is no Darwinian equivalent for indolence where all creatures are straining to compete. As a practical moralist, Malthus wished to show that the suffering produced by poverty was remediable rather than therapeutic. He was fully aware of the crucial differences between man and his fellow creatures in the animal world. Attempts to foster on to him post-Darwinian notions connected with eugenics, racism, genocide, and sociobiology are frequently a sign of the need to provide our scapegoats with a lineage.

When awarding moral prizes or penalties, much seems to turn on the degree of optimism or pessimism displayed by our heroes, though hopes unaccompanied by good reasons for hope, one would have thought, come fairly cheaply. For what it is worth, Malthus envisaged a society in which the only poverty that would remain would be confined to those 'who had fallen into misfortunes against which no prudence or foresight could provide', a society in which there were 'fewer blanks and more prizes' (E II 428). It was not visionary to encourage and expect success to attend efforts to increase food supplies ahead of population; but it was still essential, in Malthus's opinion, to issue warnings about the need for prudential restraint to achieve any permanent improvement in the condition of the mass of mankind. He described this vision as 'very cautious', concluding that

though our future prospects respecting the mitigation of the evils arising from the principle of population may not be so bright as we could wish, yet they are far from being entirely disheartening, and by no means preclude that gradual and progressive improvement in human society, which, before the late wild speculations on the subject, was the object of rational expectation. (E II 441)

He was still hoping, as in the first *Essay*, to re-establish a pre-Revolutionary Enlightenment belief in gradual improvement.

The political economist

The fluctuations in Malthus's reputation as an economist, when judged by modern practitioners, have followed much the same course described when speaking of his standing as a demographer. It has risen whenever later preoccupations have coincided, or appear to have coincided, with those which inform his work. This meant, for example, that by the end of the nineteenth century,

Malthus, though given his due as the author of some crucial propositions, shared in the decline of interest which attached to classical political economy generally. With the law of diminishing returns recognized as being perhaps permanently in abeyance, the attention paid to landownership and rents seemed excessive. Reform of the Poor Laws in 1834 and abolition of the Corn Laws in 1846 had long removed these questions from their former prominence on the agenda of British economists. Population trends and their influence on food prices, wages, and standards of living were also demoted, treated as being no longer so central to a form of economic inquiry which was increasingly preoccupied with the allocation of given, rather than augmenting or diminishing, resources. Only economists, such as Alfred Marshall, who were deeply influenced by post-Darwinian ideas on evolution, kept up the older concerns in new guise, and Marshall's interests in this aspect of economics were not passed on to the next generation.

The classical concentration on economic growth and the tripartite division of national income between the aggregate shares going to rents, profits, and wages no longer seemed relevant for another reason, namely that the behavioural assumptions which underpinned this division were less valid. Landlords were not simply and solely spenders rather than savers, the reverse of profit-recipients. Perhaps they had never been so single-minded, even in Malthus's day, though it was a common eighteenth-century assumption taken over by most of his early nineteenth-century contemporaries. Wage-earners were no longer confined to a spending role by their incomes, and their savings were beginning to be more significant than the sums deposited, with Malthus's encouragement, in the savings banks that were established to encourage working-class thrift in the early nineteenth century. In Britain at least, the rise in population had become steady rather than dramatic, and the process of *embourgeoisement* which Malthus and Ricardo had hoped for and partially analysed, was, as the rise in real incomes demonstrated, closer to becoming a reality. Comforts, decencies, and even luxuries were now part of many working-class budgets, and the whole class, or rather its male representatives, was becoming, as Malthus hoped it would, an integral part of the political nation.

With the advent of the new type of macro-economics associated with Keynes in the 1930s and beyond, there was renewed interest in the issues which underlay Malthus's dispute with Ricardo over general gluts. When Keynes decided that the doctrine underpinning Ricardian or 'classical' orthodoxy, namely Say's Law, was still one of the hidden presuppositions which made it difficult for his contemporaries to come to terms with general unemployment of the kind experienced in the inter-war period, he was naturally drawn to Malthus's challenge to this doctrine a century earlier. The resulting attempt to rehabilitate Malthus by rescuing him from the shadow cast by Ricardo and the orthodox line of thought he originated marks the beginning of the modern revival of interest in Malthusian economics. And this move was compounded by the post-war revival of interest in the economics of development and underdevelopment, where it was found that the dynamic aspects of classical thinking had much to offer that had been obscured by subsequent changes in modern economics. For these reasons Malthus's stock has been rising steadily during the last fifty years. It is now recognized that even his failures and inconsistencies were on a grand scale; that he posed many issues that are of continuing interest to economists, even if he lacked the mathematical and statistical techniques that would have enabled him to state or resolve them adequately.

This revival of interest frequently tells us more about present-day economics than it does about Malthus, though it is associated with other work in recent years which has helped us to appreciate, much better than most of his contemporaries were able to do, the relative merits of Malthus's analysis of the problems facing his own society when compared with that advanced by Ricardo and his followers. The jury is still sitting on many of these matters, but a few predictions of their verdict can be ventured. Malthus provided a better diagnosis of economic fluctuations in general and of the post-war slump in particular; his capacious, perhaps overly-capacious concept of effective demand enabled him to grasp some features of unemployment, the role of public spending, and the expansive forces needed to guarantee long-term growth prospects, better than the tidier, more aggregate supply-oriented ideas of his opponents. He also perceived some of the genuinely precarious aspects of the 'unbalanced' growth path followed by Britain during its take-off period.

But it is still necessary to return to a different kind of historical question by asking why contemporaries had so much difficulty in grasping Malthus's position, let alone its relative merits. The complaints on this score from reasonably fair-minded readers are too numerous to be ignored. Robert Torrens, for example, followed up an excessively harsh assessment ('Mr. Malthus scarcely ever embraced a principle which he did not subsequently abandon.' (PJ 265)) with one that is perhaps more judicious: 'As presented by Mr. Ricardo, Political Economy possesses a regularity and simplicity beyond what exists in nature; as exhibited by Mr. Malthus, it is a chaos of original but un-connected elements' (PJ 293–4). The same might be said of two later remarks by Walter Bagehot, namely that 'there is a mist of speculation over [Malthus's] facts, and a vapour of fact over his theories', followed by a more generous conclusion that 'he has connected his name with the foundation of a lasting science which he did not plan, and would by no means have agreed in'.

Despite Malthus's efforts to make post-Smithian political economy more applicable to a new age, he was, in contrast to Ricardo, unwilling or unable to create a new 'system' capable of commanding the allegiance of a dedicated, though small group of disciples whose writings, for a time at least, constituted an orthodoxy. Moreover, on some crucial questions of theory and policy he took a direction which had unacceptable political connotations to the Whigs and radicals who made up the bulk of the *cognoscenti* of the new science. Ricardo's theoretical system can hardly be described as an easy one to grasp, but it proved capable of being popularized and its policy recommendations were far less cluttered with qualifications. Malthus's opponents offered the application of a more straightforward logic involving free trade and competitive markets and requiring fewer, and often what seemed like *ad hoc*, exceptions to the system of natural liberty. Malthus appeared to be advancing an eclectic, idio-syncratic, even, in the case of his views on general over-production, a subversive mixture of doctrines that was only capable of being rendered systematic by later generations.

The delayed and untidy sequence of Malthus's publications and revisions to his position did not help in this regard, and some of the policies which he endorsed required detailed empirical assess-ments of what Ricardo dismissed as 'temporary inconveniences'—assessments which it was easier to call for than to carry out. Malthus's adherence to his doctrine of proportions made him both more cautious and more sensitive to the circumstances surround-ing legislative action; and this was to prove a handicap in one so committed to 'practical applications'. It enabled him to attack contemporary issues squarely and to modify his views in the light of experience. But it also led to hesitancy when he found it impossible to come up with specific conclusions that would meet his exacting criteria for locating the golden mean. A science of morals and politics so frankly vague must always be close to accepting what was expedient, or adopting a *post hoc ergo propter hoc* view of the relationship between science and the art of legis-lation. By contrast with these retrospective judgements, the Ricardian and Benthamite alternatives were more clear-cut; they seemed to promise those responsible for making urgent decisions with delivery of a prospective guide to outcomes, a set of un-ambiguous criteria for accepting or rejecting policies in advance of their implementation. That kind of confidence based on theoretical tidiness was not Malthus's strong suit, even if it is less possible, at this distance in time, to believe that this suit was capable of winning all the available tricks.

Just as some of Malthus's Whig political beliefs were beginning to seem a little old-fashioned to the new generation of Whigs that emerged in the period running up to the 1832 Reform Bill and beyond, so the same might be said of the practical moralist in Malthus, the person anxious to weigh moral and material benefits and losses in the same scale, to take account of prejudices and the state of opinion when advocating policies, invoking larger comparative and historical themes when necessary. In the eyes of more secular devotees of political economy, who were increasingly attracted by the firmer distinction between 'is' and 'ought' statements, between science and the art of legislation, Malthus's approach seemed outdated.

In all these respects Malthus was more conditioned by an eighteenth-century upbringing than many of those with whom he was dealing. The person who in 1798 had joined a debate which could be traced back to Mandeville and Rousseau, to Hume, Wallace, Smith, and others, remained very much in evidence. Hence Malthus's interest in the institutional preconditions for economic success, and his persistent concern with those moral or psychological factors which determined whether a society possessed what Hume described as 'the quick march of the spirits', the constant spark of ignition that would consistently make riches preferable to indolence. Ricardo and his followers took such matters for granted, at least as far as Britain was concerned. This Malthus was unwilling to do; economic man could not be assumed, he had to be nurtured. In theory wants might be infinitely expanding, but people had to *want* to want, and the wants had to be adapted to production possibilities. This accounts for a persistent source of disagreement with others on the subject of those stimulants that might be needed to overcome indolence, to prevent man from slowing down or falling back-wards on the path of improvement. Malthus's disagreement with Ricardo, with Nassau Senior, and others still has these echoes of his original disagreement with Godwin. The young curate who, paradoxically, made his name with an anonymous yet striking pamphlet near the turn of the century was father of the man who died in 1834.

Notes on sources

Chapter 1: the brief quotations from Marx and Engels can be found in R. L. Meek, *Marx and Engels on Malthus*, Lawrence and Wishart, 1953. The quotations from Keynes in this and the final chapter are taken from the essay on Malthus cited under Further reading. The quotation from John Stuart Mill appears in *Essays on Economics and Society*, volume I, p. 366, part of the *Collected Works of John Stuart Mill*, edited by J. M. Robson, University of Toronto and Routledge, 1963– .

Chapter 3: the quotations from Godwin are taken from *The Enquirer*, 1797, and from his *Enquiry Concerning Political Justice*, book VII, chapters 2–9, edited by I. Kramnick, Pelican Classics, 1976.

Chapter 4: the quotations from *The Crisis* are taken from the paragraphs cited in William Empson's article on Malthus for the *Edinburgh Review*, January 1837, LXIV, 469–506. Southey's comment on Malthus as a peacemonger can be found in a letter to G. C. Bedford in 1808, cited in O. Williams, *Life and Letters of John Rickman*, London, 1911, p. 148.

Chapter 7: Nassau Senior's remarks can be found in his *Two Lectures on Population with a Correspondence between the Author and T. R. Malthus*, 1829, as reprinted in *Selected Economic Writings by Nassau W. Senior*, Augustus Kelley, New York, 1966, p. 89. Bagehot's comments on Malthus are taken from his *Economic Studies*, London 1908, pp. 193–5.

Further reading

Malthus's published works have just become available in scholarly editions. There is a complete edition of *The Works of Thomas Robert Malthus* (Pickering and Chatto, 1986), edited by E. A. Wrigley and David Souden in eight volumes. For scholarly purposes, however, the second *Essay* is best studied in the edition produced by Patricia James (Cambridge, 1987), which shows all the modifications made over the period 1803 to 1826 and fully identifies Malthus's sources. John Pullen has done the same for the *Principles* (Cambridge, 1987), bringing together the 1820 and posthumous 1836 edition, as well as other manuscript material. Given the price of the Pickering-Chatto edition, it seems likely that most readers will still have to rely on cheaper editions, notably of the first *Essay* and *A Summary view of the Principles of Population* (for example that edited by Anthony Flew in the Pelican Classics series). *The Pamphlets of Thomas Robert Malthus* are available as a Kelley reprint, and were first published in 1970. A similar collection of Malthus's articles for the periodical press can be found in *Occasional Papers of T. R. Malthus*, with an introduction by Bernard Semmel (Burt Franklin, 1963).

Patricia James has provided us with the first comprehensive biography, *Population Malthus; His Life and Times* (Routledge & Kegan Paul, 1979), which, in addition to its other qualities as a guide to Malthus's life and period, incorporates a large number of previously unpublished letters. For the famous correspondence with Ricardo, however, it is necessary to consult Piero Sraffa's edition of *The Works and Correspondence of David Ricardo* (Cambridge, 1952–60), volumes 6 to 9. Of interest for other reasons is Keynes's essay on Malthus, reprinted in his *Essays in Biography*, and now as a paperback version of volume 10 of *The*

Collected Writings of John Maynard Keynes (Macmillan for the Royal Economic Society, 1972).

Much of the secondary literature is variable in quality, but a few particularly useful and reliable items can be mentioned. Despite its age, J. R. Bonar's *Malthus and his Work* (first edition, 1885, second edition, 1924, and now available from Frank Cass, 1966) is still worth consulting. W. Petersen's *Malthus* (Harvard, 1979) covers a great deal of ground, but is marred by animus towards some of Malthus's opponents. J. R. Poynter's *Society and Pauperism; English Ideas on Poor Relief, 1795-1834* (Routledge & Kegan Paul, 1969) is a classic study of its subject matter. One of the best studies of its kind is D. E. C. Eversley's *Social Theories of Fertility and the Malthusian Debate* (Oxford, 1959). For a representative sample (good and less good) of modern research on Malthusian topics by an international group of scholars see *Malthus Past and Present* (Academic Press, 1983) edited by J. Dupaquier, A. Fauve-Chamoux, and E. Grebenik. A more distinguished collection, concentrating on demographic developments since Malthus, can be found in *The State of Population Theory; Forward from Malthus* (Blackwell, 1986), edited by David Coleman and Roger Schofield.

On some of the more specialized topics covered in this book the following selection from a vast literature can be mentioned. On Malthus's theology see J. R. Pullen, 'Malthus's theological ideas and their influence on his principle of population', *History of Political Economy*, 13 (1981), 39–54. The same author has written on 'Malthus and the doctrine of proportions and the concept of the optimum', *Australian Economic Papers*, 21 (1982), 270–86. On 'Malthus, Darwin and the concept of struggle' see the article by Paul Bowler in *Journal of the History of Ideas*, 37 (1976), 631–50. An early attempt to relate Malthus's ideas on population and political economy can be found in J. J. Spengler, 'Malthus's total population theory; a restatement and reappraisal', *Canadian Journal of Economics and Political Science*, 11 (1945), 83–110,

234–64. On the changes in Malthus's position towards economic growth and manufacturing see G. Gilbert, 'Economic growth and the poor in Malthus's *Essay on Population*', *History of Political Economy*, 12 (1980), 83–96. One of the latest and most interesting treatments of Malthus's views on effective demand and economic growth can be found in Walter Eltis, *The Classical Theory of Economic Growth*, (Macmillan, 1984), chapter 5.

Index

Index